Nairobi Teasley,

One Hour 30 Minutes Defenseless...Lamb

By

Regenia McQueen-Teasley

1stBooks - rev. 09/20/01

TABLE OF CONTENT

NAIROBI TEASLEY, ONE HOUR THIRTY MINUTES DEFENSELESS...LAMB

This is a true story. The names have been changed to protect the "guilty."

Nairobi Teasley's One-hour thirty minutes defenseless...Lamb. Nairobi Teasley's unanswered "Bill of Particulars..."

Nairobi Teasley's "speedy trial"... from July 11, 1997 'til October 8, 1997, 'til December 8, 1997. Ninety days vs. 150 days. Where is due process, or the process that is due?

Nairobi was the ninety minutes, defenseless...Lamb.

On July 11, 1997, my youngest son surrenders himself. His charge—aggravated murder. The seventh month of 1997 on the 12-day, Nairobi came before Judge Speed, a judge in the Hamilton County Municipal Court. Bond was set at $500,000 cash, even though he had surrendered himself, not once, but twice.

Probable cause to hold, number one, existing warrant July 11 and observation of witnesses and police investigation saw the defendant go into and leave building immediately before and after fatal shots. The warrant has to this day never been served.

1

On August 29, 1997, Nairobi was in court for a motion to withdraw counsel. Mr. Ran withdrew himself since he felt Nairobi was not communicating with him for some reason, which I won't go into, "it is ethically impossible for me to continue to represent Mr. Teasley," said Mr. Ran.

The judge thought that I didn't want Nairobi to cooperate with any attorney that the court appointed. But I only wanted a "qualified" attorney.

He said in so many words that the questions asked were trifling stuff.

The judge asked if we were going to hire your own attorney, that is <u>going</u> to take this nonsensical test or what do you want to do? We have to move your case. What are you going to do? What are you doing? Who are these people?

I'm his mother, I stated. The judge asked can't he talk? How old are you son? Nairobi said, "I'm 19."

Can't you talk yourself, asked the judge? The judge asked what do you want to say ma'am?

I asked if he was allowed to have a competent attorney with some background.

The judge stated, "we are not subject to some stupid questionnaire that somebody made up. We don't do that. If he has an appointed counsel he doesn't qualify the counsel.

My other son, John Jr. asked can he have qualified counsel? The court asked how do we define 'qualified?'

The prosecutor asked if John could identify himself. I answered, John is Nairobi's brother and I am his mother, Regenia McQueen Teasley.

John said I am John Teasley. The thing of it is, it's not that Nairobi doesn't want counsel, or wants to be appointed counsel by the court, it's that he wants qualified counsel and he would like to have a chance to review his counsel. Is that possible?

The court: No, it's not possible.
John: Why isn't it possible?

The judge answered, "because he is his public defender. We appoint public defenders that are qualified by the Supreme Court of Ohio, and pass the bar to be attorneys. The defendants don't test the attorney that's just not done.

The judge stated if you want to hire a private attorney that you want to hassle about whether they are good attorneys or not you can do that. The judge asked John a couple of questions, and

3

John refused to answer. The judge stated, "I don't care. This is Nairobi's attorney."

I said, tell them to take you on back to jail. You don't want Norm Aubin.

The judge, "he is not saying." I said he is not. John stated for the court's record he is not saying that....

The court: you are not titled to represent him. If you will leave sire, you are not an attorney. Ma'am, you can leave ma'am. What are you doing sir? How do you want to proceed? You are not going to accept an attorney?

Ma'am, you are invited to leave, please. You are not an attorney. You are not entitled to represent him.

I said, "tell them to take you back to jail."

The court: What do you want to do sir?

Nairobi said, I want to go back upstairs.

"For the record," Mr. Ran stated, "Mr. Art and myself are private attorneys, we take appointments and cases from the court."

Mr. Ran withdraws himself from Nairobi's case. But Nairobi had also filed a motion to dismiss Mr. Ran.

So Mr. Tiger wanted all this time, would be charged to Nairobi. Which is not true.

Judge Nail stated any attorney that the court appoints is not going to be subject to your review.

So, now sir what are you going to do? You are not going to take the representation? Is that what you are saying? Nairobi, "no."

Judge Nail: We have to do something. We have to move your case and you are entitled to counsel.

So what are you going to do? Are you going to represent yourself? Nairobi said no.

Judge said I don't know where we are. I will appoint Normal Art, who will come forward. If you don't take him you will go pro se. You might set in jail until the end of time.

Judge said thank you. Put it up for disposition scheduling conference. If he doesn't want Normal Art, Normal Art will represent him, he will be here, available for him, and he will have to go pro se.

Mr. Tiger said Judge, if the record could just reflect this is because of the defender's request to dismiss Mr. Ran, he doesn't have an attorney and it would be at his request that all this time is charged to him. Nairobi never requested that the time be charged to him.

Mr. Ran's motion was granted. Judge Nail stated that Nairobi's had filed some affidavit in here, that he is entitled to—let the record reflect he had an affidavit stating he is entitled to qualify any counsel that is to represent him and that the court can't do anything about it—qualifying his counsel. This is not true.

The DSC was set for October 8, 1997. From July 11, 1997 to October 8, 1997 equals ninety days. The same ninety days given by law to bring one to trail.

Mark on the record it's at the defendant's request, he refuse to cooperate.

On September 8, 1997, Nairobi was brought to the court without notice. Every news station was contacted and was at court. One of the inmates called to let us know that Judge Nail had Nairobi in court. But he was not supposed to be in court again until October 8, 1997.

John Jr. was again put out of court for asking if his brother could have a competent attorney.

On July 31, 1997 the Sheriff Department notarized the document giving me the power to have Nairobi's court papers notarized and to file them in the Clerk's office.

I am striking all filings by your relatives, your brother and sister because they are not attorneys and they may not file papers in this case.

But the Sheriff Department gave me a notarized letter to legally file all Nairobi's papers.

Out of 6,000 lawyers in Hamilton County none want to represent you sir? Where are we going?

Nairobi for the record said, "Excuse me sir... All that information is incorrect."

So we want Mr. Art qualified. The court asked why Nairobi didn't want to have Mr. Art as his attorney. Nairobi didn't wish to answer that question. He just does not fulfill the obligations and the qualifications.

Mr. Art is the second attorney appointed by the court. "No" stated Judge Nail you had Mr. Law. But I was paying Mr. Law.

Well, what about your family filing papers on your behalf. They are not allowed to do that.

7

NO COURT DATE ON ENTRY

September 8, 1997.

The Court vs. Nairobi Teasley. Step right up, please sir. Mr. Art: Good morning your honor. The Court: Mr. Art is Mr. Teasley's third attorney and I have another motion to dismiss attorney filed by Mr. Teasley because Mr. Art wanted him to dismiss his mother and brother. Mr. Art didn't want us involved with my son's case, and John Jr. and I were not about to let this happen. The Judge: Yes, he has rights, you are right. He has a right to an attorney. He's turned him down, and now your mother and brother have helped you out. They want you to go back to jail again and you will sit there until we get an attorney—which could be forever. Is that what you wish to do sir? Yes, said Nairobi.

Now Judge Nail is mad. Okay, we need a competency evaluation. This man he felt was not competent. We will put on a suggestion of incompetence.

Nairobi said, Mr. Law, I don't know what happen to him. Mr. Ran wanted me to make statements. Statement on what? He got mad, closed his briefcase, got up and left.

I asked Mr. Art to show me identification and he didn't.

From the back of the courtroom John Jr. said, "Tell them to take you back to jail Nairobi." The judge said, okay, he wants to stay in jail.

John Jr. from the back of the court room, "what about rights? He has rights"
Set it over for 30 days said Judge Nail.

By this time the Sheriff was putting John Jr. out of the court.

John Jr. said, "This is a public place." The court said, yes, but you can't speak out in the courtroom sir. John Jr. stated we have a right to have attorneys pre-qualified. He has that right. Just like you have no right to put me out of a public place. And this man here (sheriff) is a public servant. Let the record reflect that all these continuances have been at the defendant's request and the times does not go against the State.

I, from the back of the courtroom stated, "object to that for the record Nairobi."

Nairobi said, "I object to that for the record sir. The Constable: October 8 at 9:30. October 8, not September 8, 1997. October 8, 1997 is the 90th day.

THE UNLAWFUL DEAL

What the record doesn't show is the judge and public defenders office made a deal to have a non-attorney from the public defender's office to stand with Nairobi because today was 90 days. There was no conference; no evidence was given to Nairobi. In the hallway a deal was given. We could pick any attorney we wanted and the public defenders office would pay for it. But this was just a trick. We selected Mr. Gain.

The court asked Mr. Law if Mr. Gain was to represent Nairobi in this case. Are you aware of that? Mr. Law answered, not until I came back up here this morning. Judge and Mr. Gain are on a jury view. I did speak with the family out in the hallway and told them that they would have to speak with him.

Nairobi was asked if he himself had spoken to Mr. Gain. He said no. Because he thought this was his conference. So Mr. Teasley, the judge asked, are you going to talk with Mr. Gain. Nairobi said yes.

When? Is what Judge Nail asked? Nairobi said he didn't know because this was new to him. Mr. Law said I know they are on the way back now. I just got a page.

The court knowing the 90 days to bring Nairobi to trail was today. The court should have been dismissed the case. But he set this over, and then Judge Gain would go talk to him. He asked how would we go about doing this? I mean, I don't want to make the decision. Yes sir, the judge said. This was the representative from the public defender's office that was to stand—as the non-attorney for my son, Mr. How. My name is Mr. How. First, I apologize for my attire; I was over in the jail. But my understanding from talking to the Teasley's family is that they have been in communication with Mr. Gain and he stipulated if the court would be willing to retain him on a public defender status he would explore, at least the probability of representing Mr. Teasley. Mr. Law said, I do know I just got a page that Mr. Gain is on his way back from the jury scene.

The court set this matter over for ten days for trail setting. If the judge is on this case it will be fine. Any continue of ten or more days must be agreed upon with both defendant and the court. This was not done.

The court wanted the record to reflect that Mr. Teasley refuses to cooperate with the court clinic in regard to the court's suggestion that Nairobi may not be competent to represent himself. So Nairobi refuses to talk to them. So, we are stuck with that situation. Nairobi has filed a motion to recuse without any, asking me to recuse myself, actually he used the term 'recur,' but there is not basis for

11

that.   I have a right to request that he be determined to be competent. That's my legal duty.

Now ten days.   Mr. Tiger, judge, also I, prepared a continuance entry for this **first time,** at defendant's request, for retaining counsel.

Put that entry on stated the court. **"Let the record reflect that the defendant refuses to sign the entry that continues the case for his benefit to obtain counsel."**

After this day I told Nairobi it is time to fight back. I knew now he is the Lamb. Let the Nairobi becomes the fox.

October 20, 1997.

States versus Nairobi Teasley. We are here because Mr. Teasley was going to talk to Judge Gain about representing him. Nairobi was asked if he had talked with Mr. Gain.

But instead of answering the question, this voice came and said, *excuse me Mr. Nail.* Can I say something for the record? I would like to know if you would ask the prosecutor to answer my bill of particulars and my demand for documents. Judge Nail said we need a lawyer for you sir.

I'm the one that filed the papers sir. I know, said the judge, but we are trying to get a lawyer for you so the bill of particulars makes sense to you. What do you mean? asked Nairobi.

He's going to file—he is going to answer them, all right. What else?

Mr. Tiger, Judge, what I will do is, I will answer a bill of particulars and discovery that he filed. I will comply with the Ohio rules of Criminal Procedure, but the things that he is asking for are not covered by those rules, so I will comply with the law. But what is the law?

May I proceed, asked Nairobi? Sure, go ahead, said Judge Nail.

I, Nairobi Teasley, object to everything in this court. I object to everything this court is and/or done in my case.

I object to any of the continuances being on my request. I object to whoever **forged** my name to waiver my right to an arraignment on July 25, 1997.

I am asking that this case be dismissed. My ninety days was up October 8, 1997. My family who has power of attorney to sign, **file**, and work on my case. On October 8 they were given a list of lawyers.

They have been asking for the list since July 19, 1997. They are trying to find a lawyer.

Then Nairobi explains what happen on October 8, 1997. My family was told on October 8 that the public defender office wanted a Michael Howard to be my assistant, to be counsel for me, which I objected to and they object to.

I, Nairobi Teasley, wish all my rights not be violated. Judge Nail said, very nice, okay. Now, you want Mr. Free to represent you or not, sir?

I said yes, <u>Nairobi did not</u>. Judge said, now they tell me you want Mr. Free. All right. Mr. Free is appointed to your case. Get together with Mr. Free.

Let the record reflect that Nairobi has continually refused to waive his right to counsel and has continually rejected counsel. Nairobi has already had three attorneys, which he's rejected which means that all the continuances were at his request, under Ohio case law. Nairobi objected. I know you object to everything. That's fine said Judge Nail.

Mr. Tiger, Judge can I put another continuance entry indicating he has not obtained an attorney and that the defendant needs additional time to retain an attorney?

Judge Nail appointed Mr. Free as Nairobi's attorney.

All continuance has been at his request, for failure to waive counsel.

Nairobi objected to that again your Honor.

Set for one week—October 27, at 9:30 a.m.

OUR "TIME FRAME"

October 27, 1997.

State versus Nairobi Teasley.   Last time we were here Mr. Teasley chose Mr. Free to be his attorney. *We need to put the entry of record on*, and then what's next? What do you wish to do on this case counsel? When did Mr. Free get put on the entry record? After the trail was over. But yet Mr. Free got paid.

Now, Mr. Free said, Judge flowing from that, of course, obviously we need to be thinking about ***our time frame.***

Frame is a key word.

It's Mr. Free's understanding, and to keep in mind that he was new to this problem, and that there are some <u>issues out there</u> as to whether or not time has been waived or not, based upon some interlocutory motions which apparently were made by Nairobi on his own behalf.

Mr. Free brought it to the attention of the Court, that it was going to take a while to get him up to speed to properly represent this defendant. So again, I'm asking for some guidance from the court as to where the case stands in the court's opinion as to the *time frame.*

16

The court just wanted to move on. They wanted to file a motion, hearing date. But they would go over the motions and you will have to consider what motions you need. As to the date from July 31, 1997 Nairobi had filed Affidavit of Truth on July 31, 1997, Legal Notice of Revocation of Plea with Affidavit of Support on July 31, 1997. On August 5, 1997, a legal notice of Revocation of Plea with Affidavit of Support was filed. On August 7, 1997, Image 75 the court filed a continuance without request of Nairobi, none were at Nairobi request.

On The 22nd of August, Nairobi filed an affidavit. The 25th of August Nairobi filed a letter and again on the 2nd of September there was another filing. By September 5, 1997 a Demand for Bill of Particulars and September 8, 1997 a Demand for Documents were filed.

On the 24th Nairobi filed another letter.

Again Nairobi filed on September 29, 1997 a Notice of Demand for dismissal. October 14, 1997, Mr. Law said, "file a demand to compel."

Nairobi said, excuse me Mr. Nail. I wish that Mr. Free not file any motions on my behalf. I already filed the documents. I wanted to be filed.

Judge Nail told Mr. Free that he would have to go over with Nairobi his motions. If he does not want you to file any motions, he wants you to argue his motions.

There are a lot of them in here. Nairobi spoke out, and this time for the record, I wish that, no, **I demand that you order the prosecuting attorney,** Mr. Tiger to answer my amended Bill of Particulars, Criminal Rule 7.

Court asked, answer your amended.

Could you do that sir? Nairobi asked yes or no?

His amended the court asked.

My amended bill of particulars. Did he file a Bill of Particulars, the judge asked.

Yes. I filed a Bill of Particulars under 2941.07. You filed a Bill of Particulars the court asked again.

Yeah, answered Nairobi. Okay. That's interesting. Okay. We will have a hearing on your motions. You have your lawyer; we will set a hearing down. Okay? Said Judge Nail. We will also make a finding of competency because he failed to comply with the interview. And Mr. Free, do you wish to pursue that or what do you want to do? He wouldn't cooperate.

Nairobi spoke out again. Mr. Nail, for the record, are you going to demand him to answer by Bill of Particulars?

Mr. Tiger said, Judge, I imagine Mr. Free is going to file a proper motion for a Bill of Particulars and a proper motion for a Bill of Particulars and Demand for Discovery. As I said before, the defendant's filed improperly worded motions, and he's asking for things that I am not obligated by law to give. *But he was obligated by law to give.* Mr. Tiger went on to say that he would comply with the discovery rules, the Bill of Particulars, as is mandated by law, but not the things that Nairobi was asking.

Mr. Free said Judge, just so we are making a record here today, I did interview Nairobi in the Justice Center for almost an hour and a half on Friday. One hour and thirty minutes defends in a murder case. What was said to Nairobi is it would be the logical thing for his lawyer to do, would be to amend the pleadings that he filed, to incorporate certain questions that were not asked by him, and therefore get some materials that he would logically be entitled to but were not otherwise asked for. And, I also told him that Mr. Tiger probably would be voluntarily willing to come up with some of these matters which is certainly the spirit of the rules of Discovery.

He never said what Nairobi had filed was not lawful. He went on to say that he would like to file some amended pleadings, just to (mess up things) make sure that in addition to and materials that Nairobi had.

19

Nairobi might otherwise be entitled. Mr. Tiger is indicating that he's not going to stand in the way of giving up materials once a correctly drafted set of pleadings is in front of him. Mr. Tiger was worried that if someone didn't file in the interest of the court certain documents, they would have to answer what were legal and lawful documents filed by Nairobi.

He said, "if Mr. Free is not allowed to even file any papers, how am I supposed to respond to a properly drafted Bill of Particulars motion, and Demand for Discovery?"

Nairobi knew under code 2941.07 the defendant have a <u>right </u>to file his own Bill of Particulars.

But the court asked you mean a request for a Bill of Particulars. That's what you mean, a request for a Bill of Particulars.

Is that here? He was looking through Nairobi's papers. Did Nairobi file a request for a Bill of Particulars? He didn't see one in the papers. So Mr. Tiger said Judge, I have got one. It's a demand and maybe, it's probably one of many that Nairobi has filed.

Mr. Tiger asked if he could approach the bench. The one filed August 22, 1997; it is a lengthy motion and he—.

20

Was it in the file or was it sent to you? I don't find that in the file. Demand for documents under United States Code Section 552 asked Judge Nail. So, are you Mr. Nail, asked Nairobi?

Yes, said Judge Nail. Nairobi asked again, are you saying that you are not going...

Judge cut in and said, I am looking for your motion, sir, or whatever it is. Did you file it with the Court, sir? Did you file... here?

Mr. Free said, Judge, I've got a <u>filed</u> copy in front of me dated September 5 of 1997, of a pro se demand for a Bill of Particulars.

I have it, here it is, said the Judge.

Nairobi you have to go over this with your lawyer. The code and the criminal rules set forth what shall be contained in a Bill of Particulars, and Mr. Tiger says he's going to provide you with a Bill of Particulars.

I will not comply with this Bill of Particulars.

I will not comply with this Bill of Particulars *unless the court orders me to*, Mr. Tiger said.

Nairobi asked again, "are you going to order him to answer them, Mr. Nail?"

"He is going to provide you with a Bill of Particulars, Nairobi asked. But are you going to order him..."

The judge cut in and said, "I don't have to. By law he is going to do it."

So, he is going to answer my amended Bill of Particulars, asked Nairobi.

You mean your demand for a Bill of Particulars, said Judge Nail.

Right, said Nairobi. The judge asked is there some amended motion that's in her. I am not aware of it. Nairobi answered, under Criminal Rule 7(E).

Mr. Tiger is going to give you a Bill of Particulars, just like every other defendant receives, yes.

But my Bill of Particulars asked Nairobi.

But you're what asked the Judge.

Mine, said Nairobi. Is different, answered Judge Nail.

My Bill of Particulars said Nairobi.

The judge said he is going to provide you with a Bill of Particulars in regard to this case. Just like any other prosecutor does in any other case.

Nairobi said, I am talking about mine, Mr. Free. Judge Nail asked, can you discuss...I am sure what he is talking about. Mr. Free said, I think he wants to know if his own rather unique Bill of Particulars will be answered, word for word, question by question.

The judge said, the prosecutor files a Bill of Particulars setting forth particularities of the facts that are alleged against the defendant in regard to the crimes with which he is charged. I never heard of a defendant submitting a Bill of Particulars.

Said Nairobi, under 2941.07, the defendant has a right to file his Bill of Particulars.

Judge Nail said, you take it up. I have never heard of that. You take it up with Mr. Free.

Nairobi said, it's in the book. Do you have a book here? The judge, do I have a book? Yes sir, I do. I have a lot of books. I am not going...I know you are brilliant. I can't match my mind with yours, okay. Nairobi, excuse me Mr. Nail. For the record, since you are not going to order him to answer my...

The judge cut him off and said Mr. Tiger said he is going to answer them. Mine, asked Nairobi, my amended Bill of Particulars?

Yes sir, go ahead. What are you going to do, asked the judge. Since you are not going to order Mr. Tiger to answer my amended Bill of Particulars under Criminal Rule 7(E), I Nairobi Teasley... I, Nairobi Teasley find you, Judge Nail and prosecuting attorney, Sir Tiger, are in violation of Derelection of Duty; and I Nairobi Teasley has demanded that you Judge Nail remove yourself from this case on ground that, under Code 2921.45 both judge and prosecuting attorney are interfering with civil rights and violating my civil rights.

And, under—and judge, under 2937.21 continuance, for a continuance for more than ten days, **both** the state and the accused **must agree or**. I didn't agree to any of them and I object to them.

The judge stopped Nairobi and said, let me give you a little hint. Quit filing motions if you don't want the time tolled and have accepted an attorney or waived, that's the law. Why don't you lookup the real law instead of what's in your mind, all right. We will go on and we will set this over. Okay. Can I say something else for the record, asked Nairobi? Sure, said the judge. I only had two attorneys, Mr. Nail, said Nairobi.

Judge Nail said you never had them, you refused them. Nairobi again said, I only had two attorneys, Law and Ran. The judge said there was also Mr. Art as well. Mr. Art I never filed the form for him.

You made a motion to withdraw. He was on here at one time, said Judge Nail.

Nairobi stated, but he was never my lawyer. Just like Mr. Free is never my lawyer. Okay, said the judge, you have a record.

Mr. Tiger asked the judge, I am a little confused. He is saying Mr. Free is not his lawyer? The State is going to be ready for trial as soon as the defendants wants it. Mr. Free has indicated he needs more time to prepare. I want the record to be very clear. The judge said Mr. Free is his attorney.

I object to that, said Nairobi.

Okay, said Judge Nail. So are you going to do this on your own?

No sir, I'll wait for a competent attorney, said Nairobi.

Judge said, we are back on this again. We went through this. "I made the law," you can read the Court of Appeals. You can read the case law on this. You have refused an attorney. You have a right to an attorney. It's not an intelligent waiver of attorney, so Mr. Free will be your attorney.

You may proceed any way you want, but Mr. Free will be available at all times for you, if you need the services of an attorney. All of the time that's been taken up in this case has been your constant refusal to take a lawyer.

I object to that said Nairobi. Very good, said the judge. Mr. Tiger, Judge do you want to set a date?

Yes, said the judge.

Bailiff: For trial?

Judge, yes, motions and then trial.

Mr. Tiger, we will be ready to go to trial.

Nairobi asked so is he going to answer my amended Bill of Particulars? Are you going to order him?

He is going to answer your request for a Bill of Particulars. He said he was, said the judge.

Nairobi, under Criminal Rule 7(E)? Mr. Tiger: judge, I will tell you now I will answer a Bill of Particulars. I am not going to answer the thirty questions.

Judge: I am not going to—this has gone on forever, since the implementation of the criminal rules. He has his own idea; you have your idea. You give him the Bill of particulars, you believe you owe them and you can object if—

So, what are you saying, you are not going to order him, asked Nairobi.

The Judge: He is going to do it. I am not going to order him to do something he is going to do. So, you are going to answer my Bill of Particulars, Nairobi asked.

We need a motion date, said the judge. Nairobi said, let's make this clear. Are you going to answer my own Bill of Particulars?

Mr. Tiger, what date do you want? Judge: okay. We need a motion date on this case. This is not my life's work. Get a motion date as soon as possible. We have got about 35 motions.

November 13, the bailiff said, 10 o'clock. Mr. Free said 10 o'clock. Thank you.

WHERE'S NAIROBI ON NOVEMBER 13, 1997

November 13

On November 13, there was no Nairobi. Nairobi refused to come down to court.

The Court: State vs. Teasley. All right.
The Bailiff: Do you want him sworn?
The Court: Yes, swear him in.

The Deputy Sheriff was sworn in. The judge said, yes, swear him in. The Deputy Sheriff was sworn in. All right, said the judge. Give us your name please. My name is Deputy Mat.

What is your assignment asked the judge.

I am Court Service Division, Hamilton County Sheriff's Department.

At the judge's request, did you talk to Mr. Teasley this morning?

Deputy Mat said, yes I did sir. Did he decide whether Nairobi wished to appear as these proceedings, asked the judge. Deputy Mat said he did not personally talk to Nairobi. What happened is we called Nairobi out for court, told him...told me to bring him down immediately. I went upstairs to court holding, had the jail officer call him out for

28

court. After three responses he did not reply. We then emptied out the holding tank to find him. Nairobi still did not reply.

This is when Mr. Free said he saw Nairobi. He went up to Nairobi and asked him if he wanted to go down for his hearing. Nairobi didn't want to come out for court. So Nairobi was placed in an individual holding cell.

The judge asked Mr. Free if he had talked with Nairobi as his attorney this morning?

I did, said Mr. Free to the judge. I simply asked Nairobi that question. Nairobi indicated he did not want to come down. He had nothing else to add or subtract from that. All right, said Judge Nail. The rules state that the defendant need only be present at arraignment and at trial, picking of the jury; and also at rendering of the verdict and the sentencing; unless they otherwise make themselves unavailable. And of course, we would encourage Mr. Teasley to appear be he has said through his other agents (mother and brother), and told the representative of the public defender he had no intention of appearing this morning.

By law, under the criminal rules, Criminal Rule 43, he was allowed to absent himself if he wishes at this time.

And we have to go over these motions. I am not sure; most of them really don't make a whole lot of sense.

One of them—are you prepared to argue on these motions? One of them is a motion. I mean you Mr. Free, is his representative—notice and demand for acquittal, notice and demand for dismissal; these were filed on November 6.

November 4. Notice and demand to recuse the judge. I have already overruled that. I will overrule and recusal again.

Let the record reflect that he has filed a grievance with the Supreme Court of Ohio, which sent me a letter two weeks ago that stated they found no merit in his grievance and that if he wished to pursue the problems that he presented to them he should have the right to appeal. That's what they told him, the proper way to proceed would be appeal.

The judge asked Mr. Tiger did you receive any of these, this notice and demand for acquittal under Revised Code 29(A)? Ohio Revised Code 29(A), I am not sure what that is. Did you receive that?

Mr. Tiger said, yes he had. The judge said, okay. Do you want to say anything in regard to that? Mr. Tiger: judge, I'd oppose all the motions that Nairobi has filed.

This isn't technically a motion; it looks like a notice and demand for acquittal under Rule 29(A).

I don't think any of what he says is based on the law. In looking at Criminal Rule 29, that relates to when the evidence on the case is closed, at a trial. So, Rule 29 wouldn't even apply in this situation.

The judge, Rule 29, he said Revised Code?

Mr. Tiger, he says ORC 29(A), but I would have to think he means...Judge, Ohio rules of Criminal Procedure. But that doesn't apply until trial.

He asked did you receive a copy of that? Is it served on you? Mr. Tiger: Judge, I got something in the mail. Is that it, asked the judge.

It's stamped November 6, 1997, said Mr. Tiger.
So, Nairobi did serve you. Overruled, said Judge Nail.
The next one is a notice and demand... Is that a little different than an acquittal motion? Mr. Tiger said I'm not sure I have all these documents.

Here it is, said Judge Nail, a notice and demand to strike and remove motions that might be a little different one. Nairobi has two of those, 11-3 and 11-4.
Mr. Free, this is kind of a problem. Yes Judge Nail, said Mr. Free, it is. The judge said, Nairobi

says he doesn't want you to do anything for him and he wants all the motions that you filed by Mr. Free to be removed.

But actually, Judge I only file one pleading. It was a discovery request, and in the discovery request that I filed, I specifically said that this motion does not supersede or withdraw or amend the fact that Nairobi filed his own discovery, it was in addition to his discovery request, but not in place of his discovery request.

And then, about a week later Mr. Tiger did send a lot of discovery back to myself. It's my understanding also sent it to Mr. Teasley here in the Justice Center.

The Judge: is that right?

Mr. Tiger: judge if I could ask to get something marked as State's Number 1. Mr. Tiger said Judge, even though Nairobi hasn't filed proper demands and requests, and to top it off, then I got it back in my mailbox several days ago, and its Scotch taped at the top. I have not opened it or looked at the contents in any way, but on the front of the exhibit it says, "Inmate Refused mail." It's dated and then it indicates it was "opened by mistake, contents not removed."

But also written on the envelope, on Exhibit 1, is handwritten, "answer of bill of particulars, Nairobi T CR 7-E." So, I would like to submit that to the Court and have that entered into evidence for discovery. I, on my own, decided that was the right thing to do in this case and as a result I did a very extensive discovery and a bill of particulars. I sent a copy of that to Mr. Free.

I also sent an exact duplicate copy to the defendant in the Justice Center. What I have marked as Exhibit Number. Judge: is an envelope that is addressed Nairobi Teasley with his inmate number in the Justice Center. My name is listed on the return address that was sent to Nairobi, look like on November 3, of 1997.

We will make it a part of the record that he refused the discovery that he demanded, said the judge. Notice and demand for acquittal is overruled. Notice and demand for dismissal, overruled. The recusal has previously been overruled. I will rule on it again. Overrule it again. Two days after I overruled his recusal, he filed another one. His only statement is because he's not received discovery. Then we serve discovery on him, and then Nairobi said he didn't want it. So I am not sure how are doing the wrong thing by him but he believes we did (and they did). The Bill of Particulars was filed.

Entry withdrawing suggestion of incompetence. We put that on. An entry overruling motion to recuse that went on October 29, 1997. I am not sure what other, is there a motion—then he also addressed the question, he wishes to dismiss Mr. Free. As I have told Nairobi before and Mr. Free can tell him, if he does not wish to avail himself of your services, that's fine, you can sit with Nairobi and he can be his own counsel, but I am not going to allow Nairobi to proceed without Mr. Free there to advise him. If he's willing to do so. Are you, sir? Mr. Free said, I will be on an as needed basis, if and when Nairobi chooses to interact with me.

The Court: I understand that he's being uncooperative. He tells me he is being uncooperative.

Judge: Mr. Free, when I spend my one and half hours alone in the Justice Center we get along fine. But something happened when I left. I don't know what it is. I was just asking, because Nairobi is demanding your dismissal and I am overruling that to protect Nairobi because his filings are neither completely rational nor relevant.

We overruled this—we might have to put dates on this. Did we overrule this 29 motion, this demand of dismissal?

Mr. Tiger: Judge, I don't know how many of these I got. I don't know if there are certifications on these or not.

Here is another one, called out the judge. October 31, 1997 notice of demand for dismissal that is overruled. There's no such thing—in addition, let the record reflect that under Criminal Rules there's a question as to whether we could consider any of these motions other than the one filed by Mr. Free because under the Criminal Rules the court shall not consider motions that are filed and do not contain proof of service upon the opposing party. Under Rule 49(C), all papers required to be served upon a party shall be filed simultaneously with or immediately after service.

Papers filed with the court shall not be considered until proof of service is endorsed there on or separately filed. The proof of service shall state the date and manner of service and shall be signed and filed in a manner provided for by Civil Rule 5(D). As I see it, none of these motions have that certification upon them, which is required.

Let me see now, what other motions we have. In addition, others who are not lawyers, which is an unauthorized practice of law filed some of these motions. Let me see if there are any other motions. There's a legal notice of revocation of pleas with affidavit and support signed by someone other than the defendant. An affidavit of truth, I am not sure what we are supposed to do about that. Signed by somebody other than the defendant, a legal revocation of plea. Here is another one signed by someone other than the defendant. We can't address any motion filed by someone who is not an attorney or by the defendant himself. So we don't have to put anything on for those because those are legal nonentities. So, we have one, two, three, four, five, six, seven, and eight. As I see it eight overruled. You can make a copy of this; the ones that are marked are overruled. But I was authorized to sign papers for Nairobi, my son.

Now, we have to pick a trial date.

Judge, said Mr. Tiger, did you rule on the notice—I guess that really wouldn't be motion—of demand to strike and remove motions. I'm sorry, was that a different one, said the judge?

Let's do it by date when we do these. There is one on 11/4 and one on 11/3. So we have to address each one of these, even though under the rules we are not required to.

Mr. Tiger said, overrule both of those? The judge answered, one on 10/31, too. And filing Notice of Demand for dismissal again? Mr. Tiger, I don't think I have that one judge.

Okay. This is the printout of what was actually filed. We won't consider anything that wasn't filed with the clerk, and this is a printout of what the Clerk's records demonstrate was filed.

I realize that under the rules, Nairobi did not properly file them. In order for us to create a clear record, first of all, I believe we don't have to rule on them, but if we did have to rule on them, they are overruled because they are nonsensical. So, we have to pick a trial date in this matter. Now, when are we ready to go to trial? This is well over the 90 days needed to bring Nairobi to trial.

Judge, asked Mr. Free, where do we stand on speedy trial? I would like you to clarify that issue for me. I am not sure how you interpret what the time frame is here.

Well said, Judge Nail, the defendant has filed all these motions and I am not sure we have to compute. What do you believe the time is? Mr. Tiger? asked the judge. I think he got locked up on July 11. Okay, said the judge.

And then from August 7 on, and we need to look at the Jacket to maker sure, I have marked down on my file, that all the continuances have been entries at the request of Nairobi. Nairobi never agreed to any continuances nor did he sign any. Let's get this together.

Within twelve days Mr.. within twelve days of that, and I am not sure that they have—Mr. Law filed a motion to withdraw, which I informed the defendant that it would waive his speedy trial rights. Then we try to appoint Mr. Ran and he signed an entry of continuance to August 29.

Mr. Tiger said, "right."

The judge said, "and then he withdrew, and again the defendant was told that would run against him, and that was his request that the person he discharged.   It was always at his request.

He filed the motions and anything then we appoint—there was Mr. Law, then Mr. Ran, then Mr. Art was appointed.   And Mr. Art waived until October 8, and then there was a motion to dismiss filed on September 8, and again, a motion to dismiss counsel filed and then Mr. Teasley told me he wanted a continuance because he wanted to hire Mr. Law at that time.

September 8, court date is not on the entry. So then we continued until—we kept it on—

Mr. Tiger said, I think that was Mr. Gaines, on the 90's day.

Well, said Judge Nail, first he said Mr. Law and Mr. Law was here and said he did not wish to represent him, and then he said he wanted Mr. Gain to represent him. Mr. Law was mad when he heard of this lie.

So then, October 8 (90 days) was the next date, because he wanted a new attorney. And then on, then he said he didn't want an attorney, and he filed a motion to dismiss and we set that over until October 20 and appointed you to represent him.

And again he—because—that's because he told me—Mr. Gain told me he had no intention to represent him.

38

So I believe (but we don't know) all these continuances have been against him and he is—now again he's filed another motion to have you removed, and all that time goes against him. So this rule says that—the case law says if you do anything that causes the Court not to be able to timely bring one to trial then you waive it. I think, said Mr. Tiger, that we have used 28 days for that date of his arrest on the first disposition scheduling conference. Do you wish to go over it, that was just a quick rundown and two agree that it's slightly confusing, but at all times Mr. Teasley has failed to cooperate with the Court, failed to accept any attorney that was appointed to him.

Now, Mr. Free, he doesn't want you as an attorney. I don't believe that we have done anything to waiver. We were ready. We have told him we stand ready to try this case at any time. I have been from the very beginning, Judge, said Mr. Tiger.

From the beginning, asked the judge. And of course we could not try it with all these new attorneys. You can't try it two days after you appoint a new attorney.

Now Nairobi is not cooperating. I believe he is within time. If you wish to file a motion to clarify, then we can go down the history and make a finding. But I believe the record's clear. And Mr. Teasley failed to cooperate and has prevented us from bringing him to trial within the 90 days, and in the meantime that he's wasted time from the time that Mr. Law first came on until you came on Mr. Free. He has constantly waived time by his motions and by his actions. Okay, thank you. Mr. Free said, judge do you want to pick a trial date? The Court: do you wish to talk to him before you pick a trial date? Mr. Free, well judge, I think we can pick a trial date right now. I suggest we set one within the time right now, said the judge.

That will be fine, said Mr. Tiger. Thirty days, said the Court. Okay, December 8.

FORGED IMAGE 148 AND LEGAL FIGHT

On July 25, 1997 image 148 Nairobi name was *forged* by Mr. Law's paralegal. The law is clear that no paralegal can sign or act as attorney for the defendant. This is noted for the record on December 8, 1997.

On July 31, 1997, a legal notice of revocation of plea with affidavit of support. This document was not to be construed as a normal statutory court filing conceding jurisdiction, but placed into the court record as a matter of public record.

July 31, 1997 Nairobi filed an Affidavit of Truth; this was filed for public record.

On August 7, 1997 Image 75, a continuance was entered and signed by Mr. Tiger, the prosecuting attorney, and Judge Nail. Someone other than Mr. Law signed Mr. Law's signature, but there is not a signature for Nairobi. Nairobi was not in court on this day.

Nairobi was in court July 12, 1997, then August 29, 1997, maybe or September 8, 1997.

On August 19, 1997 Image 113 Mr. Law was given permission to withdraw. He was withdrawing because of a fee different and counsel change. I was quoted $5,000, but later the fee was changed to $25,000 because Mr. Gain decided that he wanted to handle this case.

August 19, 1997, Image 114 Judge Nail appointed Mr. Ran as counsel for Nairobi.

The same day a continuance was entered on Image 159, signatures are Mr. Ran, Mr. Tiger, and Judge Nail. Nairobi never signed the continuance. On August 19, 1997, the continuance was for a DSC. On August 29, 1997, it was for a plea or trial set the eighth month, 22nd day, an affidavit was filed with the court and prosecutors office.

Also, a demand for Bill of Particulars, amended Criminal Rule 7(e) on the same date with the court and prosecutors office, comes now Nairobi Niger Teasley, proceeding in summo jure by way of special visitation and special proceeding, by and through his counsel, pursuant to Rule 7(E) of the Ohio Rules of Criminal Procedures demands the Prosecuting Attorney to furnish a Bill of Particulars which is to include but is not limited to State with particularity the exact time, place and date of the alleged offense.   State with particularity the implementing regulation as required by law that the alleged plaintiffs are attempting to impose upon the alleged defendant that makes him both liable and responsible for State with particularity the underlying statutes that imposes criminal penalties.   State with particularity each/every element(s) of the crime of alleged offense as required by law, etc.

A motion to withdraw, on August 25, 1997 was filed by Mr. Ran asking this court for an Order permitting him to withdraw as counsel for the defendant in this case. The defendant refuses to communicate with counsel, until counsel answers the enclosed questionnaire supplied by John Teasley, Nairobi's brother. Due to this refusal to communicate and other reasons counsel cannot ethically continue to represent Mr. Teasley, and respectfully requests that he be permitted to withdraw.

Entry allowing withdrawal of counsel and appointing counsel was entered on August 29, 1997. Mr. Ran was allowed to withdraw and Mr. Art was appointed to take his place.

On Labor Day, Mr. Art went to see Nairobi at the Justice Center, he told Nairobi that he was his attorney, and the family was to have nothing to do with this case. So on September 2, 1997 Nairobi "filing" requesting the immediate dismissal of Public Defender. Mr. Art for just cause not fulfilling his obligations, refuse to cooperate with defendant or client, refuse to have client's Bill of Particulars answered by prosecutor, and object to any motion filed by any attorney without Mr. Nairobi Teasley's written consent.

He, Nairobi requested to have another Public Defender reviewed, qualified.

Image 65, on September 3, 1997 is a continuance, signed by Mr. Tiger and Judge Nail to have a DSC on October 8, 1997, Nairobi didn't sign. Mr. Tiger states Nairobi is requiring a new attorney. New attorney to be approved. Defendant has filed numerous frivolous motions.

September 5, 1997 a demand for Bill of Particulars was filed again. Motion to withdraw as counsel was filed by Mr. Art.

On September 8, 1997 a Demand for Documents were filed. Demand for Documents 5USC Section 552(a) F.O.I.A.

Comes now, Nairobi Niger Teasley appearing in propria persona, proceeding in Suma Jury, by and through his own counsel demands this court to produce pertinent documents, records, any and all information in the possession of the State of Ohio pursuant to Section 552(a) the Demandant addresses this honorable court Amicus. The reasons why Nairobi Niger Teasley is making this demand upon this honorable court are the following reasons to wit:

1. The rights of Nairobi Niger Teasley have been violated: information has not been obtained; Official police report, medical examiner's report, homicide investigation report and other newly discovered information, autopsy report if any and photos.

2. Violation of civil rights of the Demandant.
3. Violation of Due Process.
4. The warrant that was supposed to be served upon the Demandant, (a certified copy of the Warrant). A request was made to broadcast, televise, photograph, record courtroom proceedings and entry granting approval was given by Judge Nail on September 8, 1997.

Entry of countinance, image 108 filed September 8, 1997 for a competency hearing signed by Mr. Tiger and Judge Nail. On this date, Mr. Art withdrew as counsel.

Image 119 was entered on September 9, 1997 for a community diagnostic and treatment center for examination.

Nairobi filed a letter on September 24, 1999 stating his 6th Amendment was being violated. He had a right to effective assistance.

The right to counsel includes the right to effective assistance thus if the appointed counsel does not meet a certain minimal standard of competence. The 6th Amendment has been violated. The 6th Amendment does not merely entitle the defendant to have a lawyer. It entitles him to "effective" assistance of counsel therefore; even a defendant who has been actually represented by counsel may show that his 6th Amendment right was violated. September 29, 1997 a notice of Demand for dismissal was filed in the prosecutors and court. Nairobi objected everything this court is doing and has done concerning Case No. B9704985.

A. Judicial order of this court is not being followed as required by law.
B. Judge Nail has waived his judicial Immunity both Qualified immunity and absolute immunity.
C. Prosecutor Attorney Mr. Tiger has failed to answer Bill of Particulars and Demand of Documents under Title S USC 552 Section (A) and Dereliction of his duty under code 2921.45 and 2921.44 of the ORC.
D. Forgery by court officer's signing Nairobi name to documents contained in Image 148 filed in Clerk Office Room 305.
E. The order of Judge Nail to have pass, present or future competency test conducted on Nairobi Teasley in which, I Nairobi Teasley object to having done.
F. Failure of the court officers on or officials to properly examine court documents submitted by police department (complaint was accurate).
G. Failure of Judge Nail to fulfil his obligation to remain natural, impartial unattached and fair to the alleged defendant Nairobi Teasley.

Mr. Art's counsel fees were approved on October 4, 1997. Judge Nail signed image 548. But Image 551 is not on the appearance report. Why?

This is a financial disclosure/affidavit of indigence, Mr. Art signed, but Nairobi did not sign the contract. Was he Nairobi's counsel?

Entered for October 9, 1997 Image 153 for continuance for October 20, 1997 signed by Mr. Tiger and Judge Nail. No signature for Nairobi.

October 14, 1997 Nairobi filed a Demand to Compel with the prosecutors and court.

Comes now, Nairobi Niger Teasley proceeding in summo jure, reserving all his rights at this time by way of special proceeding and special visitation, appearing in propria personal, by and through his own counsel, gives "notice" to this court in this pre-plea motion demanding that the counsel for the State, the Prosecuting Attorney to answer all the particularities of the Bill of Particulars furnished by the alleged Defendant. To this date, October 8, 1997, the Prosecuting Attorney has attempted to circumvent the statues by not providing both clear and unequivocal answers not merely complying (accepting and retaining the information for the record according to Black's Law Dictionary). Any attempt by the Prosecuting Attorney to answer by choice the particularities will not be accepted. The response to said Bill of Particulars or lack thereof, is wholly unacceptable, unreasonable, unsatisfactory, unwarranted, and undesirable. The refusal of the Prosecuting Attorney to answer the Bill of Particulars constitutes violations of ORC

2921.44 (Dereliction of Duty) and to maintain the judicial dignity and integrity of this court. Respectfully submitted on the 14th day of October 1997. And filed in the Prosecutor and Clerk's office.

Judge Nail on October 17, 1997 allowed for additional compensation for appointed counsel compensation for Mr. Ran.

Another continuance on October 20, 1997 was filed and signed by Mr. Tiger and Judge Nail, Nairobi didn't sign.

The reason Judge Nail and Mr. Tiger wanted to file on October 29, 1997 their demand for discovery and request for Bill of Particulars.

DATE OF MISSING IMAGE.

October 30, 1997, Image 73 for type of entry withdrawing suggestion of incompetence.

Entered October 30, 1997 Image 113 entry of continuance for November 13, 1997. Defendant has filed numerous pro se motions that need to be argued and decided, this was signed by Mr. Tiger, Mr. Free and Judge Nail, not Nairobi.

On October 31, 1997 filing by Nairobi demanding the dismissal of Mr. H. Free.

November 3, 1997 a Demand to Compel was again filed. Nairobi filed on November 3, 1997 a Notice of Demand to strike and remove motion.

Comes now Nairobi Teasley proceeding in summo jure, by way of special visitation and special proceeding by and through his own counsel, demands to strike and remove attorney's of recorded motion for the following to wit:

1. Alleged defendant Nairobi Teasley refused to accept legal counsel for attorney Mr. Free. See court transcript.
2. Alleged defendant Nairobi Teasley made it clear to the courts that he did not want any motions filed on his behalf by any attorney.
3. Mr. Free filed a request for a Bill of Particulars and Demand for Discovery without (Caveat and Gravamen) Nairobi Teasley's written consent. The alleged Defendant herein challenges the jurisdiction and persona jurisdiction of this legislative tribunal in the above-mentioned captioned colorable case. Failure of the courts to strike and remove this motion from the courts recorded file, will constitute a violation of ORC Section 2921.45, ORC Section 2921.44, Title 18 Section 241, ORC Section 291.45, ORC Section 2921.44, Title 18 Section 241 and Title 18 Section 242. Further, by such failure by the Judge, shall be construed as constructive entry of nolle proseque causing

the immediate termination of this instant case.

November 4, 1997 a Memorandum of Law in support of notice and demand to recuse Judge Richard A. Nail for Bias and Prejudice.

MEMORANDUM OF LAW

I.

The statutory language of the Ohio Revised Code governing both Civil and Criminal Procedures in courts in Ohio is quite clear: "If it shall be alleged...that the judge is prejudiced...the court shall call in another judge to sit on the cause." The word "shall" means impiration or mandatory. (Black's Law Dictionary, Ed. Pg. 1375. Once a judge has stepped outside his jurisdiction. As will be the case here should the court refuse to "get off the case" then he is no longer in excess of jurisdiction: he is in total absence of jurisdiction, which may lead to the interesting question, does any Articles in the Ohio Constitution (a remedy for every injury) abrogate the common law rule of judicial immunity? The State in its Constitution may supercede and abrogate the common law (US vs. Harrison County 399F 2d. 485 (5th Cir 1968).

II.

The Court's bias is easily seen from the asseverations from the Recusant attached hereto; Code of Judicial Conduct (as adopted by the Supreme Court of Ohio, effective 12-2-73) Canon of Ethnics described herein:

Canon 1: The type of conduct engaged in by the court described herein amounts to fairly low standards of judicial conduct (See Court transcripts for verification).

Canon 2: The court showed that its opinions rather than subscribing to references in/at law to take precedence over court procedures. The Recusant's confidence in the judiciary at this time has eroded appreciably by irresponsible and improper conduct by said judge and Prosecuting Attorney.

Canon 3: The court is swayed by its own partisan and personal interests, not the law.

1) The court allowed ridicule costing dispersions at the recusant not only in front of his immediate family, but also in front of witnesses, and other condescending remarks leveled at the Recusant, to take the place of order and decorum.

2) There is absence of a proper and qualified prosecuting attorney in this case. To this date, said judge has attempted to "shield" the prosecutor from faithfully executing his

duty by remaining silent and not answering the Bill of Particulars prescribed by law.

3) Ohio Revised Code and Section 2941.07 provides as follows:

Upon the indictment or information is vague, indefinite, uncertain or insufficient the court is required, as a matter of rule and statutory law, to grant the (alleged) defendant's motion for a bill of particulars. Such a particularization of the elements of the alleged crime is not discretionary with the court, it is <u>mandatory.</u> State vs. Petro, 148 Ohio St. 473 (1947).

This document does not represent or construe the recusant's personal opinion but based on first hand knowledge and experience. It appears that the Prosecuting Attorney and the court are not practicing law but practicing malice with impunity. Justice in this case is dilatory, expensive, uncertain, and remote. The deliberate attempt by the judge to circumvent and to defeat the statue prescribed by law makes said judge an adversary rather than an advocate of the law. The recusant can no longer maintain public confidence in said judge and the court by their willingness to evade their fiduciary responsibilities, duties, and obligations. It is the recusant's position that recusal would be a far more expeditious remedy than the other remedies that the court would find available. Wherefore, recusant moves that the Honorable Richard A. Nail to excuse himself from case No. B 9704985.

On November 4, 1997 John Jr. and I, Regenia served for Nairobi to the prosecutor's office and the Common Pleas Court Notice and Demand to recuse Judge Richard A. Nail for Bias and Prejudice.

Comes now Nairobi Teasley herein after Recusant, Advocate of the Law, by on behalf of himself, proceeding in Suma Juce, by way of special proceeding and special visitation, waiving none of his Secured and Substantive rights give notice and moves the Hon. Richard A. Nail to recuse himself from this action for the reason that said judge has demonstrated bias and prejudice on behalf of the State of Ohio. The action of both the Prosecuting Attorney and said judge can most accurately and charitably be described as sickening. See the asseverations of the Recusant and the Memorandum of Law.

Then the Notice and Demand for Acquittal ORC 29(A), was filed November 6, 1997.

It says, comes now Nairobi Teasley, advocate of the Law, by and on behalf of himself, proceeding in Suma Jury, by way of special proceeding and special visitation, waivering none of his Secured and Substantive rights, appearing specially and not generally, conferring no jurisdiction to this honorable court to find a judgment of acquittal pursuant to ORC 29(A) for the following reasons to wet:

53

1. That the complaint is defective and insufficient and the facts stated therein were not properly presented to support a finding of probable cause such that a valid Warrant (within the meaning of the 4th Amendment) could issue.

2. That the complaint brought forward by a law enforcement officer must be based upon the officer's first hand knowledge and may not act as the complainant when he/she is alleging knowledge of the commission of a crime when that "knowledge" is not based upon his/her own observation and knowledge, but instead is based upon the observation(s) or knowledge of others.

3. That the factors of "probable cause" as within the 4th Amendment must be "supported by Oath or Affirmation of the complaint.

4. That the only individual(s) who are lawfully competent as complainants are those who directly and actually observed or who have the first hand knowledge of the event(s) constituting the crime.

5. That the complaint the prosecuting attorney is relying upon is "information" which is not properly verified (meaning properly notarized or otherwise sworn to) complaint(s) is constitutionally deficient, unless the prosecuting attorney himself (or herself) is actually a first hand witness to

the act or acts constituting the crime alleged.

6. That the contents stated in the complaint constitutes prima facie evidence and void on its face. Furthermore, the information contained in the complaint constitutes and improper pleading at law.

7. Any Oath or Affirmation asserted by any individual who is not a first hand witness and who merely claims to be a proper complainant in lieu of the actual witness(s) thwarts the provisions of the 4th Amendment as well as raises particular questions as to the 6th Amendment right to be confronted with the witnesses against him.

8. That the complaint fails to State a claim upon relief can be granted."

9. That the proper parties in the issue have not been properly "joined."

10. That there has not been any formal joining of the issue(s).

11. Lack of "due process of Law."

12. That the alleged defendant was not properly advised of his legal/lawful rights.

13. That a properly served Warrant was not served upon the alleged defendant.

14. That the speedy trial provision in the statutes has been criminally violated, forcing the alleged defendant to remain unlawfully incarcerated.

15. The "true party" of interest who is making the claim has not been identified. The

party pretending to be is wholly ficticting heding under a corporate name.

16. The prosecuting attorney has not been held in contempt of court for not furnishing the answers to the Bill of Particulars as required by Law.

17. The complaint has not stated the "nature" of the claim that it is making by the alleged plaintiff(s).

18. The party making the original complaint has made and reached a "legal conclusion" a law which is strictly prohibited by the Law.

19. The complaint has not defined the causation of harm of the alleged crime.

20. The complaint has not defined or identified the "actus reus" of the alleged crime.

21. The complaint has not identified or defined the "mems rea" of the alleged crime.

22. The complaint has not identified or defined the "concurrence" between the "mens rea" and the "actus reus" of the alleged crime.

23. The complaint fails to specify whether the alleged crime signed by the complainant is categorized by either a "general intent" or "specific intent."

24. The complaint fails to specify or define the concatenating circumstances that led the complainant to believe that the alleged defendant committed the alleged crime.

25. That the contents in the complaint are nothing more that an averment of a legal conclusion and not a statement of

issueable facts and has not been treated by
this court as a statement at all.
26. There has been no evidentiary hearing.
Wherefore, the alleged defendant prays to
this honorable court to grant this Notice
and Demand and to judge the facts stated
herein and to render a consciousable and
judicious decision in the interest of Justice.

Respectfully submitted by Nairobi Teasley,
incarcerated citizen.

John Jr. and Regenia for Nairobi filed a notice of
objections on the 4th day of November.

November 14, 1997, Judge Nail and Mr. Tiger
set a trial day for December 8, 1997 entered a
continuance.

On November 18, 1997 a notice and demand of
dismissal was filed for Nairobi by his brother John
Jr. and his mother.

Also on November 14, 1997, Judge Nail signed a
court security order for John Teasley: The Court
has reason to believe that John Teasley, an
employee of the Hamilton County Juvenile Court,
presents a serious security risk due to the threats
of violence he has made in connection with the
criminal proceeding against his brother Nairobi
Teasley had been disruptive during court
proceedings and has espoused support for the anti-
government positions held by the "Freeman"

organization. Therefore, the Court orders that Mr. Teasley's Hamilton County Employee's ID, be confiscated by Juvenile Court until the Criminal charges against Nairobi Teasley have been concluded. Mr. Teasley will then be requested to go through the ordinary courthouse security measures.

On November 13, 1997, midway into the motions hearing John Jr., and his mother Regenia, walked out of the courtroom. We have told Nairobi he was not to be present. So, there was no reason to stay. This made the judge **mad.**

On November 18, 1997 John Jr. and myself filed a Notice of Objections for Nairobi. It says, comes now Nairobi Niger Teasley, advocate of the Law, by and on behalf of himself, proceeding in Sunimo Jury by way of special proceeding and special visitation, waiving none of his secured and substantive rights, conferring no jurisdiction to this court, gives Notice to this court of the alleged Defendants Objections to the entire counts proceeding held on November 13, 1997 by Judge Nail, Prosecuting Attorney Sir Tiger, and attorney Herbert Free.

Pursuant to Criminal Rule 43 the alleged defendant elected not to be present in this particular stage before trial due to the fact of the prosecuting attorney Sir Tiger's contributory negligence to answer the Bill of Particular filed by Nairobi Niger Teasley, as stated in the Order and

Demand to compel. The courts throughout the entire court proceedings beginning at the arraignment to this time, has consistently and deliberately demise the alleged defendant access of having his legal documents signed and/or filed in the courts file. Clerks office, prosecutor's office room 411, etc. The courts have not indicated any STATUTES or Regulation(s), barring a non-attorney to give legal paperwork to the alleged defendant to aid in his defense.

Certification of Service, I Nairobi Niger Teasley certify that the true original of the forgoing Notice of Objections has been served on 18th November 1997, AD by delivering this original to the office of Clerk of Courts, Prosecuting Attorney of Hamilton County.

Cc. Ohio Supreme Court Disciplinary Counsel, Ohio Supreme Court, United States District Court.

Again on November 18, 1997 a Demand for Bill of Particulars Amended: John Jr. and Regenia filed Criminal Rule 7(3) for Nairobi.

On November 19, 1997 Judge Nail filed an entry overruling defendants notice and demand for acquittal ORC 29A filing.

Ohio matter came on upon defendant's filling and the court, being fully advised in the premises overrules the filing. The defendant was given an opportunity to fully argue or present evidence on this filing. The defendant chose, voluntarily and of his own free will, not to present any additional evidence in support of this filing. Signed by Judge Nail, Mr. Tiger and Mr. Free.

On November 20, 1997, Nairobi filed Notice of Objection to strike and overrule the court motion. On December 17, 1997, Notice of Objection filed by Regenia because John Jr. was arrested.

December 2, 1997, a Notice of Alibi Rule 12.1 was filed. Notice and demand to quash the indictment.

A. The court acting on behalf of its own selfish interests by way of Sua Sponter and depending on the ignorance of the Demandant impaneled the Jury in the absence of the Demandant. This being done violates Criminal Rule 43(A) which says that the Demandant is required to be present. Furthermore, the Demandant never waived his right either expressively or implied.

B. Upon searching the records of the court, there is absent any "true bill of indictment since all members of the Grand Jury (homage) are not named individually.

C. There is absent the total number of individuals that is required to be properly impaneled (i.e. 6,12,15) including the majority that is required to reach an indictment.

D. That the so called "true bill of indictment" in the court record at this time is fraudulent, misleading, spurious, and unlawful.

E. The court relying upon Criminal Rule 4(A)(1) could not issue if the members of the Grand Jury have not been impaneled properly thereby arriving at a majority consensus to obtain an indictment.

F. The complaint, defective for various reasons, is prima facie evidence of an alleged crime. The Grand Jury cannot possibly reach an indictment without knowing fully the essential facts of the alleged crime and the "elements" of the offense required by Law.

G. That an initial appearance of the Demandant cannot take place for the following reasons:

   1) That the Demandant has not been informed of the "nature" of the accusations against him Rule 5(A)(1).

   2) That the Demandant has been denied "suitable counsel" that said Demandant can rely upon counsel's professional knowledge and experience. The counsel(s) appointed by the court has been both hostile and arrogant. Rule 5(A)(2).

Wherefore, the Demandant prays to this court to seriously consider this matter and will correct this matter in the interest of justice, maintaining confidence in the Judiciary and public safety.

Certificate of Services

I certify that a true, convict and expect copy of the foregoing document entitled Notice and Demand to quash the Indictment has been hand delivered to the clerk of courts on the two days of December 1997. Nairobi Niger Teasley, Demandant.

December 4, 1997, the State's Supplemental Response to defendant's Demand for Discovery. Now comes the State of Ohio, by and through its assistant Prosecuting Attorney, Sir Tiger, and supplements the discovery previously given as follows.

1. Evidence Favorable to Defendant. A witness, Janet White, said she saw the defendant shortly after 10:10 p.m. on the night of the offense on Ezzard Charles Drive. She indicated he was wearing red shorts and no shirt and was riding a bicycle that he put into his apartment on Ezzard Charles Drive. Shortly after that, he left alone on foot.

December 17, 1997. Notice and Demand for Nairobi's mother filed acquittal ORC 29(A) and C. On December 23, 1997. Rule 33 New Trial Affidavit was filed.

1. Irregularity in the proceedings or abuse of direction by the court because of which the

defendant was prevented from having a fair trial.

2. Misconduct of the jury, prosecuting attorney, or withers for the state.
3. That the verdict is not sustained by sufficient evidence or is contrary to law.
4. Error of law occurring at the trial.
5. The judge and prosecutor violating my civil rights.
6. To not having my DSC or 10-87997 which is in 8-29-97 transcript.
7. To not having my Bill of Particulars answered.
8. To the prosecutor Sir Tiger being seen going in and out the jury room while the jurors was trying to reach a verdict on 12-12-97.
9. To not having a competent attorney.
10. To not being arraigned cause my name was "forged" on legal documentation image 148.
11. To not having a speedy trial under the 6th amendment.
12. To the judge overruling my acquittal under Rule 29A and C renewed.
13. To Herbert Free filing a Demand for discovery and Request for Bill of Particulars and he is not and was not my attorney.

There was a felony sentencing findings filed December 22, 1997.

Compensation for Mr. Free was $4,500.

November 19, 1997 Judge Nail overruled defendant's notice and demand for acquittal ORC 29A filing image 26. Defendant's notices and demand for dismissal dated November 16, 1997. Image 27 Defendant Notice and demand to recuse Judge Nail, image 28. Image 29, defendant's memorandum of Law In support of Notice. Image 30 defendant's notice of demand to strike and remove motions dated November 13, 1997. Image 31 defendant's Notice of demand to strike and remove motions dated November 4, 1997. Image 32, defendant's demand to compel dated November 3, 1997. Image 33, defendant's Notice of demand for dismissal, dated September 9, 1997. Image 34 Nairobi's notice and demand for dismissal dated October 31, 1997. Nairobi on November 20 filed two sets of objections.

On November 26, 1997, the State filed a supplement response to Nairobi's demand on November 28, 1997 Subpoena were issued for a number of people. I was a witness, but I never got a subpoena. The day of the trial I was asked by Mr. Free to be a witness. My daughter was given a subpoena the day before the trial started to be a witness a witness for her brother.

Eight subpoena for witnesses were returned and endorsed by December 1, 1997.

On December 2, 1997 a Notice and demand to quash the indictment was filed for Nairobi and

Notice of Alibi. On December 4, a motion to view the premises was filed. The Jury was impaneled and sworn on the 8th of December 1997. More served subpoena on December 9, 1997.

On December 8, 1997 both my sons were in court. On this day I had to go from one courtroom to another for my sons.

John Jr. was arrested for supporting his brother Nairobi. He also lost his job. On this day the cause progressed with the first day of testimony. This went on through the 12th. On December 12, 1997 the Jury verdict of guilty of aggravated murder, we further find that the defendant did have on or about his person, or under his control, a firearm while committing the offense of aggravated murder, we further find that the defendant did have on or about his person, or under his control a firearm while committing the offense of aggravated murder and displayed the firearm. Brandished the firearm, indicated that he possessed a firearm or used it to facilitate the offense of aggravated murder.

On December 29, 1999, an entry appointing appellate counsel Chuck Ham.

January 2, 1998 an entry overruling notice of objection filed 12-17-97 was filed January 14, 1998 a Notice of appeal was filed by Mr. Chuck Ham.

On January 23, 1998, entry allowing withdrawal of Counsel Norm Art, and appointing as counsel, Herbert Free. The trial was over. Why was Mr. Free being appointed <u>after</u> the trial?

An amended Notice of appeal was filed on 2/9/98.

On **January 29, 1999** a judgement entry was filed after the trial was over and the appeal filed.

The court speaks through their entries. Image 209, when was Mr. Free appointed? (January 23, 1998.)

When was Judgement entry? (Image 63).

?Praecipe to forward the judgement entry filed January 29, 1999 ?nune pro tune to December 22, 1997 to the appeals case to become part of the record, signed by Judge Nail. April 30, 1999 Judgement Entry and decision affirming judgement of trial court.

On June 18, 1999 copy of notice of appeal of appellant Nairobi Teasley: filed in the Supreme Court of Ohio on June 14, 1999.

September 10, 1999 a petition for post-conviction relief pursuant to ORC #2953.21. On September 9, 1999 Motion to dismiss untimely post conviction petition filed September 10, 1999.

On October 15, 1999 a notice of appeal filed No C990722 copy sent to Hamilton County Prosecutor.

November 15, 1999 Nairobi Teasley filed a docket statement.

February 18, 2000 Nairobi's attorney Bill Gall filed a docket statement March 30, 2000. Also on November 22, 1999 a motion to re-open appeal pursuant to Appellate Rule 26(B).

Now comes appellant, through the undersigned counsel, pursuant to appellant Rule 26 (B), and respectfully request that this Court re-open the appeal of his conviction and sentence in case No. B 974985. There exists a meritorious issue not presented to this court due to the ineffectiveness of appellate counsel. There is good cause for the late filing of this motion.

Doug Man represented appellant on appeal. As this Court is aware, Mr. Man took leave from the practice of law due to an extremely serious illness that is life threatening.

So much so, the court was forced to reassign numerous appeals assigned to Mr. Man this past spring. Mr. Man was retained by Nairobi's family to represent him on appeal. It was not until over thirty days past the mandate had issued in the original appeal, that appellant's family was informed of Mr. Man's illness and inability to proceed further on Nairobi's behalf. An issue does exist in appellant's appeal, which has merit. In demonstrating the merit of this issue, appellant must show that the failure to raise the issue rests on the ineffective assistance of Counsel. State vs. Murvahan, 63 Ohio St. 3d 60 (1992). Appellant is not required to show the result, would have been different, but for the ineffective representation. He is <u>only</u> required to show there exists a reasonable...

None of the circumstances listed on (B)(1) through (4) apply in this cause.

1) If the testimony will relate solely to an uncontested matter.
2) If the testimony will relate solely to a mater of formality and there is no reason to believe that substantial evidence will be offered in opposition to the testimony.
3) If the testimony will relate solely to the nature and value of legal services rendered in the case by the lawyer or the firm to the client.
4) As to any matter if refusal would work a substantial hardship on the client because of the distinctive value of the lawyer or the firm as counsel in the particular case. What is clear is that trial counsel violated his ethical obligations in this matter.

This is not a question that is left to the discretion of trial attorney. Continued representation by the lawyer violates this disciplinary rule. In addition, when a lawyer is faced with a situation when the rules will be violated DR 2-110 calls for a mandatory withdraw: "A lawyer representing a client before a tribunal with its permission, if required by its rules, shall withdraw from employment and a lawyer representing a client in other matters shall withdraw from employment. If he knows or it is obvious that his continued employment will result in a violation of a Disciplinary Rule."

Trial counsel <u>never</u> made the motion to withdraw. It was obvious that continue employment would violate the rules. Even Nairobi, a non-lawyer, recognized the problem when he objected to Free's representation during trial. "I already told you he was not my lawyer because he u/m, you know what I'm saying he filed stuff on my brother so that would be like a bias toward me." (TR p. 515).

Counsel's failure to withdraw calls into question his entire performance at trial. An objective observer must now question the strategy of not interviewing witnesses before trial, not viewing the scene, not investigating the case, no possibility the result may have been different. State v. Bradley, 42 Ohio St. 3d 136 (1989) Nairobi contends burden is met by following issue. A violation of the Disciplinary Rules is in itself ineffective.

Argument:

Nairobi's right to effective representation under the sixth Amendment to the United States constitution and Article I Section 10 of the Ohio Constitution are violated when defense counsel is a listed victim in an indictment relating to the matter on trial and fails to withdraw from representation.

In the matter at hand, defense counsel was a listed victim in an indictment alleging Nairobi's brother John had conveyed a threat of his life rotating to counsel's representation of Appellant Counsel did refer to the indictment at the start of the trial (TR p 58). However, counsel did not advise the trial court he had made a full disclosure of the facts and that he would likely be called as a witness in the trial of his brother.

Additionally, Appellant was never called upon to consent to the continued employment. Instead, Nairobi continued to dismiss his counsel. (TR p 65).

DR 5-102 controls what a lawyer's obligations must be when he learns that he may have interest that could impair his professional judgment.

It mandates the attorney to withdraw from representation. This does not create a discretionary call on the part of the lawyer. Disclosure by the lawyer that he informed his client that he did not initiate the action does not alleviate his duty to withdraw.

"If, after undertaking employment in contemplated or pending litigation, a lawyer learns or it is obvious that he or a lawyer in his firm ought to be called as a witness on behalf of his client, he shall withdraw from the conduct of the trial and his firm, if any, shall not continue representation in the trial, except that he may continue the representation and he or a lawyer in his firm may testify in the circumstances enumerated in RF 5-1-1(B)(1) through (4)."

"John Teasley was indicted in Hamilton County Court of Common Pleas No. B 978987 with intimidation against Free, the judge, and the prosecutor for threats of bodily harm made in the hallway outside of the courtroom" conducting cross-examination, not objecting to improper arguments by the prosecutor, not requesting a curative instruction after repeated improper questions by the prosecutor.

One can only come to one conclusion when it is viewed in that light. Trial counsel's performance fell way below the recognized standard. Strickland v. Washington, 466 715 668 (1984).

Wherefore, Nairobi prays that this court re-open the direct appeal in this matter and order that a briefing schedule he issued in order to brief the argument presented herein.

A brief for Nairobi was filed May 11, 2000 in the courts of appeals first appellate district Hamilton County Ohio.

June 14, 2000 Brief for Appeal was filed.

On October 14, 2000, an appeal must be filed with the Ohio Supreme Court. By November 30 the "Habeas Corpus" must be file.

'Habeas Corpus' (Latin-that you have the body.) The popular writ to preserve personal freedom, directed to the person in whose custody a person is kept, ordering the body of the person so kept to be brought before the court issuing that writ, so that judicial inquiry may be made into the legality of the restraint or imprisonment and appropriate judgment rendered there on.

Due Process
My sons...I was blessed with two
John Ray Sanders Teasley Jr.
and Nairobi Niger Sam Teasley

Where is due process, or the process that is due?

John Jr. was arrested on November 25, 1997, and Nairobi surrendered himself on July 11, 1997. Both trials started on December 8, 1997 for John Jr. and Nairobi in different courtrooms.

This is a true story about John Jr. and Nairobi.

WHAT IS A BROTHER

This book I have written because of things/lawless things that happen to my sons. Some time people must find your weakness... But then your weakness _must_ become your strength. No matter what happens one _must_ continue to do what is needed to get the "project" completed.

A quitter never wins and a winner never quits.

You guys _are_ from the bloodline of the 8 Lords Proprietors.

What is a brother...

A brother is some one who's been where you've been who knows you and what you're about... Someone you know you can call if you need to when something's just not working out. A brother is someone who's more than just family... his friendship is one of a kind.... And the closeness you've shared through life's laughter and tears is the deepest that you'll ever find.
From Charles II We Are All That Are Left

And to "all" the other brothers—that helped. Thank you from the bottom of my heart. Pastor John, Mr. Gaines, Mr. Harris, Mr. Lawson, Mr. R. Thompson, Mr. Mansfield, Mr. Reif, Bill the Printer,

74

Nairobi Teasley,
One Hour 30 Minutes Defenseless...Lamb

Mr. Mansfield, Nairobi, John Jr. Mr. Gallanger, and the Mallory's, etc.

JOHN TEASLEY...AM I MY BROTHER'S KEEPER

On November 25, 1997, John Jr. was arrested on William Howard Taft Road. There was and still is no arrest warrant. He stayed sixty plus days in jail for supporting his brother.

The judge, prosecutor, attorney, and Mr. Howard all were subpoena to court. This I'm told was the first time in Hamilton County that a judge, prosecutor, and attorney have to be in court (for pulling) together for the appeal of Nairobi.

Things that were said by the above people clearly show how bias they all were in the case of Nairobi Teasley. The one hour thirty minutes defenseless...Lamb (Nairobi) and intimidation of John Jr. November 13, 1997.

On January 1998, John Jr's trial started.

After the jurors were seated, the trial of my son John Jr. started. Mr. How testimony began.

Judge Marie Ann, stated, "okay Mr. Right, you may call your first witness."

Mr. Right said, "thank you," and Mr. How was called.

76

He gave his name, who he worked for, and how long he had worked for the public defender's office.

Mr. How stated that he was a mediator and interview clients. Mediation means that I work in direct relationship with the court whenever we have cases that need any kind of a mediation.

Doing the questioning Mr. How answered one of the questions, as really, I was in Talbert House as a client because I had some legal problems in my past.

He worked for the public defender's office. But he had a record of aggravated robbery, and a felonious assault which was part of the same case. He spent seven years in penitentiary.

He had gotten a government clemency. But later he had a forgery in '93. This time he was not confined, he got something else. He was assigned to the case of Nairobi Teasley.

He stated that he was assigned to Nairobi in August or September, when really it was October 8, 1997 he was going to stand with Nairobi as his legal assistant. There was a perception on John and his mother's part that there was an undercurrent or de facto atmosphere in the courtroom of unfairness in relationship to the case, the judge, and the prosecutor.

On October 28, Judge Nail overruled some motions, said Mr. How. John Teasley and Ms. Teasley were quite upset because they were overruled and felt that that was unfair. John felt that his way to respond to that was to act disruptive or to act out in the courtroom. I advised him against that. At that point I told him that it wouldn't serve Nairobi Teasley any good, and it might put him at risk in terms of being arrested, or bring his employment into question.

Did he observe John's behavior in court, the question was asked.

Yeah, and outside the court. Outside the courtroom what behavior did you observe on the part of Mr. John Teasley that you felt required your services. The question was asked by Mr. Right.

Mr. How answered, you know, the vague references to what recourses that he had available to him in terms of rectifying what he thought was unjust and unfair.

Mr. Right said, let's talk about November 13, 1997. Outside the courtroom? Yes sir, said Mr. How. Outside Judge Nail's courtroom. This was a pre-trial matter that was up that day.

The prosecutor on this case was Sir Tiger. The defense attorney was Mr. Free. Mr. Right asked Mr. How was there behavior on the part of John Teasley on that date that you felt required your services as a mediator. Yes, was Mr. How's answer.

Mr. Teasley said Judge Nail was illegal, Sir Tiger was illegal, and the attorney Mr. Free was illegal. And that since they didn't want to resign from the case, then he was going to bring some people in to act illegal to get them off the case. They were going to proceed illegally, also. That was his statement. He said they underestimate people that I have outside of Cincinnati who can come in here and act just as illegal as they act.

Mr. How also stated he felt he should report what was said to the judge, prosecutor, and attorney, which he did. This is what caused John Jr's arrest on November 25, 1997. He spent ninety (90) days in jail, all because a criminal lied on him.

John Jr. never had a criminal record in his whole life.

January 22, 1998 the court called Mr. Tiger to the stand. Having been first duly sworn, was examined and testified as follows:

He gave his name, Mr. Tiger. His job was assistant prosecuting attorney. He was a team leader in the Common Pleas Division. He also was the supervisor for four attorneys. He was in three different courtrooms. He also travels from courtrooms to courtrooms to handle special cases. He is a practicing attorney since 1978.

Mr. Tiger had Nairobi's case from the very beginning. He was in charge of interviewing the witnesses, putting the case together, presenting it to the grand jury, it was his from the start to the finish. He was the one handling the case.

Mr. Tiger was asked if he remembered the date of Nairobi's arrest on the case. It was believed sometime in early or mid July 1997.

Do you remember, if you know, the last day for trial on the case, the ninetieth day? Mr. Tiger answered the ninety day limit was up. Mr. Lily, John's attorney objected. Mr. Right was given the chance to have Mr. Tiger answer the question. Mr. Tiger said, the trial was December 8th of 1997, which was for in excess of the ninety-day period. In fact, that was a point of dispute on the defendant in saying we didn't try him in ninety days, but because of the delays attributed to him, that ninety days was extended. So, I think it would have been up sometime in October. Mr. Tiger was asked if John had any disruptive behavior in the courtroom. Mr. Tiger answered, yes, I'd have to say there were two specific courtroom instances that I can recall. Normally, and I know in Judge Nail's room, when the judge comes out from his or her chambers, the bailiff or the constable raps their gavel and asks everybody to stand. John wouldn't stand, which was a sign of disrespect, to me. Mr. Lily asked for this statement to be stricken. And it was.

After he wouldn't stand, the defendant comes before the bench or the judge and stands, let's say right here, in front of the judge. I'd be over here, or somewhere in the area. And there's a discourse between the defendant, the judge, myself, however, that's going to go. John Teasley was disruptive from the back of the courtroom. The judge told him to be quiet; he wouldn't be quiet. In fact, when a judge tells a person, in this case, John Teasley, in open court to stop what he's doing, I would have thought he'd stop, but John didn't. Mr. Lily objected, but it was overruled.

Mr. Tiger said there were motions filed by Nairobi Teasley and/or his family in the case that I handled against Nairobi Teasley. The question was to Mr. Tiger, by Mr. Right. "Were you responsible to respond to those motions?

Mr. Tiger said, Nairobi wanted me to. John Jr., was charged with intimidation, not courtroom behavior, not anything to do with anything but statements allegedly made by Mr. Teasley to Mr. Howard on the 13th of November, as conveyed to the judge. At that time, there was nothing in the indictment, nothing in this case at all that has anything to do with the trial of Nairobi Teasley and those proceedings.

The judge states, "my understanding, based on what I've heard so far of the defense in this case, is that any statements that might have been made were made in the context of removing the attorney and the judge in the normal course of business, and not through any violent means. And if that's the position your client's taking, then how the proceedings moved along are relevant to whether, in fact, that's really what he meant by all of this." Mr. Lily said, I understand that, but we're talking about what Nairobi Teasley has done, and that has nothing to do...

Now, if you want to talk about what my client did, that's why I objected to the question, did Nairobi Teasley and/or his family...

Well, let's limit it, said Judge Marie, a certain amount of foundation needs to be laid.

Mr. Right asked Mr. Tiger, "during your course of representation of the State as the prosecutor in this case, there were motions filed that you had to respond to?" Mr. Tiger answered, yes. Mr. Right asked, did you have a problem with some of those motions? Yes, I did, answered Mr. Tiger.

Normally in a case the motions are filed by the attorney, and there are standard motions for discovery, for bill of particulars, for what evidence you intend to use, to express statements, and there's a certain way that an attorney will do that, and the wording that they'll use. In this case, there was an abundance of motions filed, but those were filed by Nairobi in handwritten form. There were a lot of them. Just did not—they were very lengthy; page after page after page of things that didn't have any pertinence to the case at all.

Did Mr. Teasley, John Teasley, at any time criticize you or your handling of the case, if you know? asked Mr. Right.

Yes, said Mr. Tiger. He approached me in the hallway of this floor of the courthouse and basically followed me down the hall asking me what was a statute number. And I believe it was 2941.07, I think, right off the top of my head. He came up to me and said, "what's 2941, and I think it was .07. And I was, I don't know.

And he was asking me if I was familiar with a bill of particulars, what are they. And this was another home of contention. One of the motions that you're referring to that the defendant felt— Nairobi Teasley felt he had a right to know all of those things. In fact, one of the motions for bill of particulars, which is what this man asked me about in the hallway at the end of that filing. What the motion said was that if I didn't do what they wanted I was subject to unlimited personal liability myself, and that other motions along those same lines indicated that I forfeited my right to be a prosecutor if I didn't do it the way, you know, they wanted me to do it.

Mr. Tiger was asked to select the particular pleading that he's referring to.

The state marked it exhibit Number 1. Mr. Tiger selected another and it was marked exhibit Number 2.

One was a demand for bill of particulars, which I signed for Nairobi and John Jr. and I served to Mr. Tiger on August 22, 1997. Mr. Tiger did not respond. Mr. Tiger looked again at exhibit Number 2, it was a notice of objection filed by Nairobi Teasley. Nairobi is saying he wants to notify the court of this timely objection to the prosecuting attorney, Sir Tiger, bill of particulars, and discovery. Said bill of particulars is unacceptable, vague, unclear, and without merit. It appears to the alleged Nairobi that the bill of particulars from the prosecuting attorney is nothing more than transcendental legal nonsense. By not answering the bill of particulars, the prosecuting attorney has forfeited his right to serve his position, a prosecutor attorney.

On January 26, 1998, exhibit three was marked. This was a transcript of two different proceedings in court. One was August 29, 1997. It was a motion of one of Nairobi Teasley's to get off the case.

Were you in court on September 8, 1997 Mr. Right, asked Mr. Tiger. Mr. Tiger said yes. In front of Judge Nail, and was there a court reporter present, asked Mr. Lily. Yes there was, answered Mr. Tiger.

Mr. Lily asked, did you have an opportunity to review exhibit 3? Yes, I have, answered Mr. Tiger. Is it accurate in terms of what you recall from those proceedings? Yes, answered Mr. Tiger, as far as the words that were said, yes it was. And was Mr. John Teasley disruptive in any way on either or both occasions?

What makes him disruptive to one person wouldn't be to another. Let's talk about November 13, 1997. The information communicated to you by Judge Nail, or anyone else, relative to something that was said out in the hall. And did Judge Nail counsel with you individually with respect to that information? And as a result of receiving that information, how did you react? Mr. Lily objected because judge, he's trying to get in the back door what he can't get in the front door. The objection was overruled.

Mr. Tiger notified the supervisor of the law enforcement agency. I told him exactly what had happened. I told him that I was in fear of my life and my family's life. I got his cell phone number and pager. I asked him to have very heavy-duty patrols around my house. Two or three different law enforcement people came to my house and spoke to my wife. I had to keep it from my children because I didn't want them upset. I got all the cell phone numbers of all the officers that were on patrol. I normally would keep my garage door or car door, or door unlocked, a lot. I never do that any more. I keep a very close eye on my kids, and just make sure everything is very secure and locked all the time. And basically, keep an eye just on myself and my surroundings, just to make sure there's nothing suspicious as far as I could tell going on at any time.

What affect, if any, did this information have on you as you conducted the Nairobi Teasley's case, asked Mr. Lily. Mr. Tiger answered, "I prosecuted Nairobi Teasley to the best of my ability." I can't say that I backed down to him or that I changed any kind of strategy. I was just as aggressive as I would have been had I not heard that However, again I was very cautious and careful in the hallways, on my way home, and to and from my office. I never knew when or if an attack was going to happen. But in terms of the actual courtroom when I was in the courtroom I did what I had to do as far as what I thought the right thing to do in that case was, and that's what I did.

The courtroom was full and some of the same people are in the courtroom today. And that constantly was on my mind throughout the course of that trial.

The question was asked, "when did you start the Nairobi Teasley trial?" I believe it started December 8, 1997. So the threat **preceded** that **trial**. Yes, Mr. Tiger answered. There were a number of people in the courtroom. And there were times when Mr. How, Judge Nail, Mr. Free and myself were all in the courtroom together. And I did speak to both Judge Nail and Mr. How about what was said. Mr. Lily asked Mr. Tiger how long had he been a prosecutor, and Mr. Tiger answered fifteen years. And you've made a lot of people unhappy during the course of that prosecutorial career, have you not? You've been in a lot of courtrooms where families of people on trial have been disruptive, have you not? It's not uncommon, is it? Yes, was Mr. Tiger's answer.

The question was asked of Mr. Tiger, "Do you think disruptive means threats?" Answer from Mr. Tiger was, "In this case I do." Well, like I said before, John Teasley didn't have to go through security, the way I understood it. He doesn't have to go through the metal detector because he had some kind of pass because he worked for the court system. And he'd follow me down the hallway before... One time? One time answered Mr. Tiger. It was asked, is that correct? On your way to the courtroom, is that correct? asked Mr. Lily. Right, it was in his face the way he asked the legal questions. But I didn't answer John's legal question.

Were you afraid of John? I was afraid of him, answered Mr. Tiger. How much do you weigh? And how tall are you? He answered around 225 pounds and six-four. A man of your size is afraid in a courthouse with all the security guards around? Yes, I am, answered Mr. Tiger. With weapons, you could be a five-foot person killing a seven-foot person. And the handgun that was used in this case was never recovered. But Mr. Tiger, you never ever, ever, ever, saw John Teasley with a handgun or any other kind of weapon of any kind whatsoever, did you, asked Mr. Lily.

That's true answered Mr. Tiger. Mr. Lily asked, "You saw no signs whatsoever that my client, John Teasley had any kind of weapon whatsoever, did you? Mr. Tiger answered no. Mr. Lily asked, all right, at no time did my client, John Teasley threaten you in any way, shape, or form, did he. Never direct, by what was told to me, answered Mr. Tiger. What he told me, and what communicated to Judge Nail also, stated Mr. Tiger. You don't know of your own knowledge anything that my client may or may not have said; isn't that correct? My client's mother, Regenia Teasley never made any kind of threat of any kind to you at all, did she?

Mr. Tiger answered, she did in a—after Nairobi was found guilty there was a hearing where she came up on the witness stand and under oath told the judge that she had seen me two times come out of the jury room while the jury was deliberating, which was an absolute lie. She said that under oath. And she also said she had a handgun in her house, as well. Again nothing was said directly to me by her, that's correct. Mr. Lily asked, and on one in the Nairobi Teasley's case issued any kind of threat at all towards you personally, did they? No words were spoken to me, said Mr. Tiger. By anyone? No.

The question was asked of Mr. Tiger, no one brandished or displayed a weapon in front of you? That's right answered Mr. Tiger.   Did you see anything, asked Mr. Lily?

My movements, I mean it's pretty easy. I mean we all work around here.   I don't know if somebody's following me to my car. I don't know if they know where my car is. I did see some of the people involved in this case outside of court when I was walking to my car. I don't know what they've done.

They have to leave the courthouse too, don't they, asked the Lily.   Sure, answered Mr. Tiger. Are you suggestions they can't be in the public streets while you're there?   His answer was, you know better than that.

Did you receive any threatening phone calls at home or office?   Did your wife receive any threatening calls or letter or anything of that nature during this, did she?   No, answered Mr. Tiger. So, except for what Mr. How told you, you have no reason to believe that there were any threats made to you or your family? All right. Mr. Teasley, Mr. John Teasley was upset at legal counsel, legal representation, his brother was receiving, is that correct? Is that fair to say? He did not believe that either you or Judge Nail had the proper authority to act in prosecuting and trying his brother; is that correct?   Did he not

89

express those feelings during a hearing in the case of Nairobi Teasley? Yes, he did answered Mr. Tiger. Mr. Lily went on to ask, and he also said that the judge and you and the defense counsel at some point or another ought to be removed from the case, isn't that correct? Mr. Tiger said, it was very clear to me. Mr. Lily, said just answer the question, please yes or no.

What was the question again? The question was asked, and Mr. Tiger answered yes. And it was very clear—if I could explain that—that whenever Nairobi Teasley was in court he would be very hesitant to answer anything, and before he did he'd always look back o the back of the courtroom, and there John Teasley would be. And he'd be the one, John Teasley, calling the shots as far as what he should say, how the case should proceed. John Teasley was advising his younger brother, is that correct? Yes. All right and he was advising him to ask that judge and you and the defense attorney be removed from the case. And there's nothing illegal about removing a judge, prosecutor, a defense attorney, from a case, is there? If it's done correctly there's nothing improper about it, is there?

I never really heard of a prosecutor getting removed from a case. I've heard of judges recusing themselves if they know a party, if they know a witness, for those reasons, but I've never heard it done the way—the defendant—this defendant wanted it done. Let me ask you this,

Mr. Tiger, are you familiar with the civil rights cases that arose in the southern states in the United States of America back in the 1960's? Generally, was his answer. Were you aware of certain times when United States Marshals would go down into some of those southern states and, in fact, remove judges and prosecutors and defense attorneys from cases. And removal of those officials from state criminal cases down there at that time would have been against those state's laws wouldn't it? I don't know answered Mr. Tiger. Basically, a judge can remove themselves from a case, it's just called recuse, recusal, the implication would be that the judge maybe couldn't see it as impartially as he could if he didn't know any of the parties. And as a result, a judge would step down from a case, and it would be sent to another judge. And judges can be removed from cases by the Supreme Court of the State of Ohio? Yes, they could. It happens sometimes upon the finding of what we call an <u>affidavit of bias and prejudice.</u> I've heard of affidavits being filed, I think it's extremely rare that one is granted. Oh, but they are granted, Mr. Lily asked. Yes, but I don't know how often answered Mr. Tiger. And in that case, if a judge were removed from bias and prejudice that would mean the judge had probably refused to step down him or herself, right? Right answered Mr. Tiger.

So they're being removed by an agency other than themselves, are they not? And if they refused to step down upon an order from the Supreme Court, they would be removed by force, would they not? Asked Mr. Lily. Mr. Tiger answered by force? By force if necessary, said Mr. Lily. Mr. Tiger said he had never seen this happen. But there is a procedure there in the law. Mr. Tiger said he didn't know what the procedure was, I've never had a case where a judge has been forced by the Supreme Court to step down when they didn't want to.

Well, said Mr. Lily, you're very fortunate, I have. Now, you made much of the fact, in your testimony the other day that this case went on for some time, the case of State of Ohio versus Nairobi Teasley; is that right? Mr. Tiger answered, I wouldn't say I made much of it. It was reset a number of times. Mr. Lily asked, is it usual for a capital murder case to be reset many times? This wasn't a capital. I'm sorry, said Mr. Lily. Its life in prison answered Mr. Tiger. Mr. Lily asked, is it usual for those to be continued a number of times, it is not? I'd say yes, Mr. Tiger answered. Because the defense has not had the opportunity to prepare the case prior to indictment; isn't that right, asked Mr. Lily. That could be one of the reasons, answered Mr. Tiger.

Later during the trial, Mr. Right asked Mr. Tiger if there was an affidavit of bias and prejudice filed in the case of Nairobi Teasley. Yes, Mr. Tiger said, there was. There was—I don't know if it was titled that, but that was the content of what was filed. Mr. Lily asked Mr. Tiger if he knew whether Regenia Teasley or Nairobi Teasley filed the affidavit. It wasn't filed by an attorney; it was filed by Nairobi. What we call a pro se motion? Right. Was it acted upon? Mr. Tiger answered, the Supreme Court said that everything was being done right, and that Judge Nail should hear the case.

Question from Mr. Right. "Was there ever a request that Judge Nail recuse himself?" I don't know if that word was used, but they wanted him removed from the case. Well, recusal wouldn't be frightening to you, correct? Recusal would not affect me at all, if that's fine, thank you. Would an affidavit of bias and prejudice frighten you? No, said Mr. Tiger, but you went to your local police agency and told them something and got all their phone numbers, didn't you? It wasn't a lawful removal that you were concerned about, was it? No, answered Mr. Tiger, like I said. I was extremely scared, and let my wife know immediately what was going on—and we did what we could to prevent an attack the best that we could.

January 22, 1998 Judge Nail's appearance was requested.

The judge later stated for the record, "well then, of course the right to counsel was very important. John Teasley and Nairobi and Nairobi's and John's mother were up there, and they...when I sought to appoint someone to replace Mr. Ran, they said that they were entitled to a qualified attorney. And I said, yes, you are. And the two qualifications are that they have passed the bar and that the public defender has approved them to represent murder cases, aggravated murder without capital specification, because everyone is not—the Supreme Court makes the public defender qualify people to represent in certain cases, like aggravated murder a capital offense, that's not really that important.

But they insisted John and his mother that a qualified attorney would have to fill out this questionnaire. I said that's not true, you know, I'm going to appoint an attorney, and they are not going to be required to fill this out.

They became vociferous about it. And I had to ask them to take their place in the back. And I think John and his mother both yelled out, "just go to jail, they're not doing the right thing by you." and I told them they had to leave that they could not. They wanted to file papers in objection to my filing. I said you can't do that, you have to be an attorney to file papers. Even if you're related you can't practice law. They insisted they were going to do it. The judge was handed exhibits 3 through 7. Very important was exhibit number 2. Judge, let me hand you now what's been marked as Defendant's Exhibit 2 for identification, and ask you if you can identify that for us, please? The judge answered, it looks like the appearance docket for the case of State of Ohio versus Nairobi Teasley. And it's a printout of **all** the filings in the case. I

don't know that it's all, but—it could be. If you say
it is, it ends—**it would seem to be the end**
because the last thing is an appeal.

Questions from Mr. Lily, "and that's a printout of
all docket entries and the entries filed in the case
of Nairobi Teasley, is that correct?"   The judge
said, "I would presume it is. I haven't reviewed it."
Mr. Lily asked, "if to your knowledge." Judge, "of
course I'm sure that the court **only** speaks through
its entries, is that correct?"   "In regard to legal
decisions, yes," the judge. (this is very important).
Review that exhibit, if you will judge, and
determine whether or not Herbert Freeman was
ever appointed as counsel for Nairobi Teasley,
asked Mr. Lily.   The judge answered, "there are
some subpoenas issued here. At least this doesn't
demonstrate an entry has been filed. I don't know.
I didn't look at it. I didn't review the papers. I
mean there could be an entry that's not on the
docket. I'm not saying there is, I'm saying there
could be."

Mr. Lily asked, let me hand you..."I've handed
you a packet of papers, judge, and ask you to
identify that packet of papers I've handed to you,
that you're looking through now. The answer given
by the judge, "I see a number of entries filed by
Mr. Free, or signed by Mr. Free, motions filed. No,
I **don't see on in here** for appointment of Mr.
Free." Mr. Lily asked, "and when you say you don't
see one, you're referring to the fact you've just
reviewed the entire file jacket for the case of the

State of Ohio versus Nairobi Teasley; is that correct?

Yes, answered the judge. Mr. Lily asked and that's the case about which we've been talking all morning; is that correct? Yes, answered the judge. Okay, said Mr. Lily, I take it, it would be fair to conclude then by the fact that you cannot find an appointment of Mr. Free as attorney for Nairobi Teasley, either in the printout of the docket or in the case file, that in fact, **he never was officially** appointed as attorney for Nairobi Teasley, would that be true?

The judge agreed no entries of record. If you say officially appointed, I don't know.

Mr. Lily asked, the court speaks through its records. I think you're already told us? at any rate, Mr. Nairobi objected to being represented by Mr. Free, didn't he? Judge Nail said, "Nairobi objected to being represented by anybody, including Mr. Free." Mr. Lily asked, "he wanted to represent himself did he not, at least at one point." The judge answered, "he made various statements. I asked him if he wanted to represent himself. I told him I didn't recommend it, buy he had a right to do it. And at one time he said he wanted to do it. Then he'd change his mind and say he wanted an attorney." And I said Mr. Free is your attorney, and you can cooperate with him or not. He will be with you during the trial.

Actually judge, said Mr. Lily, if I may direct you. What? asked the judge. To Rule 65, the Supreme Court rule that governs the qualifications of attorneys in capital cases refers only to capital cases, not non-capital cases. Judge said, right. Mr. Btrigari presented me with what he told me was the public defender's list of people his office felt were qualified to try aggravated non-capital murder cases. Mr. Lily said if I told you Mr. Btrigari was mistaken, you would not disagree with me, would you? I didn't check it out, said the judge.

Now Mr. Right starts questioning Judge Nail about the appointment of Mr. Free. Now, you were asked to go through that court file from the clerk's office, and there was no entry in their appointing Mr. Free as counsel? Yes, said the judge. Mr. Right asked, is this the **<u>first</u>** time in your experience as a judge that an entry didn't find its way into a file? The judge answered, "I daily find papers in other files that belong...I mean, we normally put one on, and it either didn't make it in the jacket, or... I don't know. I don't have an explanation. But I agree with Mr. Lily, **<u>no entry</u>** appears on the docket, and no entry appears in the file jacket. But Mr. Free acted as his attorney. I'm not sure what the point is." Mr. Free actually many times reported that he got along with Mr. Teasley until we got in court.

Mr. Free, actually in that file, has several motions or pleadings with Mr. Free's name on it? Yes, and continuances and motions, answered the judge. Mr. Right asked, "now you indicated that Nairobi Teasley at times would suggest that he would like to be his own lawyer?" "Yes, answered the judge. And then at other times he would ask for an appointed counsel? As he would put it, a qualified lawyer said the judge. And involved in this interchange between Nairobi Teasley and the court, the family was also involved in the selection process of the attorneys, said Mr. Right. The judge answered Mr How and Mr. Btrigari believed that the only way this could be resolved was through a discussion with not only Mr. Nairobi Teasley, but also John Teasley and Nairobi Teasley's mother. Because they had—it arose from the situation that every time I addressed Mr. Teasley in regard to an attorney—his right to an attorney, his desire for an attorney, he would turn around and consult to the bad of the courtroom with his brother or his mother. Okay. And it became clear that he was relying upon their counsel, said Judge Nail. Mr. Right said, "if I know you well enough Judge, I'm sure you wanted to get this show on the road? Well, I mean yes; the defendant has a right to a speedy trial. He has a right to an attorney. All these confrontations came by my insistence that his rights be given. I did not understand it at all.

He **one** time asked on **October 8**, 1997 for a continuance to obtain Les Gain as an attorney. Ninety days on October 8, 1997, the defendant has a right to a speedy trial. He has a right to an attorney. Nairobi **one** time asked for a continuance to obtain Les Gain as an attorney.

Nairobi on October 8 was asked to sign a continuance on his ninetieth day. But he objected.

Mr. Right asked, well looking back on the whole situation—the activity of the family and the different and inconsistent positions taken by Nairobi Teasley as to whether he wanted a lawyer or if he wanted to represent himself—did you have the feeling that you were being jerked around a little bit?

Judge Nail answered, "I believe that the...the system can be used if you keep objecting and refusing attorneys, even though they're qualified. And I had concerns that if it became commonplace that every defendant could pick his court appointed lawyer, the whole justice machine would grind to a halt, because we would never be able to accomplish anything. And the point is that a lot of defendants believe that court appointed lawyers are somehow lesser lawyers, and the truth of the matter is that it's not true.

Mr. Right asked, I believe we can agree, and you've been asked, Mr. Teasley did not directly threaten you? No, he did not, answered the judge. But you felt that it was necessary or prudent to take steps to **deny** Mr. John Teasley access to the courthouse by means of his courthouse identification? We have judicial educational courses for threat, said the judge. Now, Mr. Lily asked the judge, Judge, did Mr. Nairobi Teasley ever ask for the appointment of a specific lawyer?

He had, said Judge Nail. He had expressed interest in having Judge Gain be his lawyer. Wait a minute, now. I'm listening, said Mr. Lily. The judge said, and I had asked Judge Gain, who was there, whether he was willing to undertake the representation of Mr. Teasley, and he said not on an appointed basis. So he didn't direct—he made a request for a continuance to talk—that he was interested in retaining Judge Gain to be his attorney. And Judge Gain happened to be in the room. And I asked him if he would be willing to represent him, and he said not on an appointed basis. Judge, are you aware the **Revised Code of Ohio** permits defendant to request specific attorneys to represent them? asked by Mr. Lily. Okay, answered the judge. You and I have disagreements about this list.

Mr. Lily asked, I'm not speaking about the list. Generally speaking, the State of Ohio does permit an indigent criminal defendant asking for a specific lawyer to represent him and be paid by the State and the Court?

The judge answered, "Sure, I have a problem with that!"

Mr. Lily asked, that's why I'm asking you whether Mr. Nairobi Teasley asked for a specific lawyer to be appointed to represent him? Only indirectly, when he talked about retaining Judge Gain said Judge Nail.

Mr. Lily asked, you might or may not know this, "is the Teasley family close?" To each other? asked the judge. Yes, said Mr. Lily. It would seem, said the judge. Mr. Lily asked, and was Mr. John Teasley, his brother, and Ms. Regenia Teasley, his mother, concerned about the son's trail? I have no quarrel with that, said Judge Nail.

Now, its January 26, 1998 and the testimony of Mr. Herbert Free. Mr. Free stated, back on October 24, 1997, I officially replaced prior counsel in the Teasley case. So, I picked up Mr. Teasley's case, let's say mid-stream.

Mr. Right asked, were you retained or appointed by the Court? Mr. Free said yes, I was appointed on October 24.

Now, was that appointment, were you compensated by the public defender's office on an appointment like this? asked Mr. Right. The answer was what happened is you keep track of your time, and you submit your bill to the local public defender's office, and they submit it to Columbus.

Mr. Right asked, you don't work for the public defender's office, you're compensated through that office? Exactly, said Mr. Free.

According to my notes, I spoke to my new client the same day I was appointed. He was in the Justice Center at that time; and then three days later on the 27th I met with **prior** counsel.

Eventually, on November 6, I'm showing on my notes that I was called by John Teasley, and basically he was asking me to withdraw from the case. He had philosophical differences between the way I was handling the case and the way he wanted the case handled.

The question was asked how long was that after you were appointed?

The answer from Mr. Free was I was appointed on October 24th and he demanded, if you will, that I withdraw on November 6, 1997, about two weeks later. I had filed some discovery in the case, some requests for information from the prosecutor's office that I felt we were entitled to.

I was trying to correct some matters that had been asked for by my client in his own behalf. My client was filing pleading pro se, or by himself. The only problem with, that is, not being an expert in the law, he was, if you will, screwing it up. So I amended those pleadings. And John Teasley's call was essentially a complaint that I shouldn't have done that.

Mr. Right asked Mr. Free, okay, now did the court at any time in Nairobi Teasley's case allow Nairobi Teasley to act as his own attorney? The arrangement, Mr. Right, that we had on October the 24th, or when I was appointed was that given the fact there was a history of three other attorneys of record that had not been able to get along with the defendant, the **arrangement** at that point in time was that I **pre-agreed** with the judge on the record that **if** the defendant chose to use me as his lawyer, I would interact as his lawyer. And **if** he chose me not to act as lawyer the judge wanted me still to sit there because it's his experience, as well as my experience, that people who are distrustful of the system feel that they need a lawyer when trial comes around. As so he wanted him to have a lawyer, even though he might change his mind later on.

So I agreed to sit there, hopefully as his lawyer in an active way, but otherwise to be there should he change his mind later on.

Clearly, you were appointed by the Court to represent him, asked Mr. Right.
Yes sire, said Mr. Free.

Did the court ever appoint Nairobi Teasley's mother to act as his counsel? How about John Teasley? Did the court ever appoint John Teasley to act as his lawyer? No, said Mr. Free. In fact, there was some—the court was specific in trying to make sure that only lawyers would be involved or the defendant in his own behalf, those are the only people with status. You can practice law in this kind of case with somebody helping you if they're a lawyer, or you can represent yourself, but not by yourself, if you're not a lawyer.

The question was asked did you withdraw from his brother's case when requested to do so? Mr. Free answered, well, I was polite, but I reminded John Teasley that the conversation that I had on the record with Judge Nail back on October 24th that our deal, if you will, was that I was going to be there on an *as needed basis* even if the defendant chose not to need me, but I wasn't going to withdraw. The Judge didn't want another lawyer to accept the case and then file a motion to withdraw the first time things got a little rough.

First of all, it isn't a good plan, simply from Nairobi Teasley's standpoint, to be involved in a trial when you're not interacting with counsel. Because, of course, just like in sports, you're going to be unprepared when a matter comes up. But there were certain safety concerns that were related to me by...

On the 13th when I showed up at a hearing that I thought was supposed to just deal with these pre-trial motions, first thing I learned was that Nairobi Teasley was refusing to come down from the county jail annex, which is on top of this building. And then after I went upstairs and tried to straighten that out, I came back down and then at that point in time I learned from a combination of Mr. How and from Judge Nail that things apparently had been said by Mrs. Teasley and John Teasley that would be reasonable to be perceived as being threats against the judge, against Sir Tiger, who was one of the two lawyers I was up against as lead counsel and against myself.

Mr. Right asked, "were you intimidated by the information you received?" Well, the first thing I asked said Mr. Free... No, just answer my ...were you intimidated? asked Mr. Right. Yes, sure, Mr. Free answered. Now, will you explain your answer? asked Mr. Right.

Mr. Free said, "If these allegations were true, they would cause you to have concern of risks for your personal safety or for that of your family. Did you tell your wife, Mr. Free?" Yeah, Mr. Free answered.

Well Mr. Tiger, who represented the prosecution, was in the same meeting. And I felt that if the government had an interest in the case he would certainly be the logical person to evaluate and do anything on that end. But I didn't want to be perceived as being—doing stuff contrary to my client's best interest. But at the same time, I didn't want to be insecure in my personal life, said Mr. Free. Mr. Right asked "well, did these feelings stay with you during the course of the trial?" Yes, they did said Mr. Free. All of us were pretty careful to try and simply avoid contact with the family, to try and avoid any confrontations, sure, something that normally wouldn't be a problem. It's typical to try and get along with your client's family, and not to try and avoid them.

Did this hinder your work and your handling of this case, in your mind? asked Mr. Right. Certainly, answered Mr. Free. Because usually on a charge like this, just given the bond problem, your clients' usually locked up. And since you're not on a budget like the O.J. defense team, you need to use your clients' family as your arms and your legs to try to run down information. It deprived me of what is normally a resource. It meant I had to do more myself. It meant I had to do more guess work. And it created a problem in the sense that...the issue of trust was more of a problem because of the bad chemistry between myself and Regenia and John Teasley, respectively, that it would have been had they simply stayed neutral on the issue and told Nairobi to try and work with me and try and trust me as best as he could.

So you had your fears during the conduct of that case, asked Mr. Right. Yes, I had answered Mr. Free.

Did Mr. John Teasley ever threaten you directly?

He threatened to sue me for malpractice on November 6,said Mr. Free. Mr. Lily now has the floor.

Mr. Free, you would agree with me that a court speaks through its entries, would you not? Certainly, probably, that's the case, yes, said Mr. Free.

Mr. Lily said, let me hand you what's marked as defendant's exhibit number 2 for identification, and ask you if you can tell us what that is?

Mr. Lily, this looks like a computer printout of the items that get entered into the court's journal as the progresses.

And what case would that represent, asked Mr. Lily?

The caption on the top is State of Ohio versus Nairobi Teasley, and the case number is B9704955, said Mr. Free. Now, said, Mr. Lily is that the same case that you have purported to represent Nairobi Teasley? Yes sir, it is.

Could you find for us, please where in those docket entries you were appointed attorney for Nairobi Teasley?

I'm showing that on September 8 of 1997 Mr. Art withdrew and an entry went on reflecting that he withdrew as counsel for Mr. Teasley, and the case was continued until October the 8th. I can't tell just off the top of my head whether my appointment is reflected on this.

Well said Mr. Lily, take your time and find whether or not such an appointment in reflected in that record. I don't see it Mr. Lily said Mr. Free.

Would you accept my word that it **doesn't** appear in that case at all? You're a man of your word, I'm sure you looked better than I did.

Let's go back to your appointed—**so called** appointed representation in the case of State of Ohio versus Nairobi Teasley. You began acting on his behalf on October the 24th; is that the date you said Mr. Lily? That's the date I'm showing in my own notes, said Mr. Free.

At any time from October 24th onwards did Mr. Nairobi Teasley accept you as his counsel? asked Mr. Lily. There were times during the trial when he gave me the green light to do things for him, there were times when he didn't. Between October 24 and the trial date which was, I believe, December 8 when the trial started. Mr. Free answered it was December 8, which was a Monday, and it ran all week, yes.

Between the time of October 24 and December 8 did Nairobi Teasley ever say he wanted you to act as his counsel? Mr. Free answered actually, it was the other way around. There were times when he said he didn't want me to act as his counsel.

And you continued to act on his behalf?   Mr.
Free answered in the fashion I indicated before.

Mr. Lily asked, and he during that time filed
motions requesting that you be removed as his
counsel, did he not? Yes sir he did, said Mr. Free.
And yet you stayed on the case? As I described
earlier, yes I did. When you say as you described
earlier you're referring to the agreement you and
Judge Nail had that you would sit by as an advisor
whether he wanted you or not, asked Mr. Lily.

That's correct.   The judge's theory was that
even though Mr. Teasley did not want to be
represented by me, at a certain point that he might
change his mind during the proceeding. And he
wanted someone available who was competent in
the field so he wouldn't be out on a link. So, said
Mr. Lily you would not disagree with me, would
you, that Mr. Nairobi Teasley had an **absolute**
right to represent himself? I think you're probably
right in that Mr. Lily.

Mr. Free, all right. But at any rate, you did not
withdraw officially.   Did you withdraw unofficially
from the case? No.

On November 6 I did talk with John Teasley
when he called me and that was the day he
threatened to sue me for malpractice, and
demanded that I withdraw from the case. But I did
not withdraw. Nairobi wanted me on in the initial
portion of the case. When I filed these discovery

pleadings that were where there was a problem. So Nairobi and I had a problem between the 24th of October and the 13th of November.

Mr. Lily asked, did you have any court appearances between the time of October 24 and November 13, 1997, in this case?

Mr. Free answered, "I'm not showing formal court appearance on this particular sheet." Did you have other than a telephone conversation with Mr. John Teasley on November 6, did you have any other telephone conversations or meetings with him, face to face meetings, prior to November 13?

I don't think so said Mr. Free. How about Mrs. Regenia Teasley, did you have any conversations with her either by telephone or in person between October 24 and November 13? Did you ever see Mrs. Teasley or John Teasley in the courtroom prior to November 13, 1997? Did you ever see Mrs. Teasley or John Teasley in the courtroom prior to November 13, 1997? I'm not exactly sure, said Mr. Free. I understand that. How did you know which was which, if you didn't talk to them or they weren't introduced to you, asked Mr. Lily. Usually Regenia Teasley would be with John Teasley, said Mr. Free. Some of Judge Nail's people identified them to me.

I think, Mr. Lily said, that you testified that you liked to use family members to assist you when you represent criminal defendants, particularly in serious cases, is this correct? Sure, answered Mr. Free. But you never attempted to use Regenia Teasley or John Teasley between the time you were put on the case by Judge Nail and November 13? I'm not sure I did, answered Mr. Free.

Did you not think, did you not consider that it might have helped you communicate with Nairobi Teasley by forming a good relationship with John and Regenia?

Certainly on November 6 when John called me, and that was the day he threatened to sue me for malpractice, and demanded that I withdraw from the case. But you did not withdraw asked Mr. Lily. That's correct, said Mr. Free. I told him that I would be there on an as needed basis, and I told him that Nairobi needed to make the decision whether he wanted to be represented by me or whether he wanted to represent himself. And I think you already told us Nairobi wanted you off the case? Certainly at that point he did, yes.

But you Mr. Free continued on? Yes I did Mr. Lily. When I filed these discovery pleadings, that was where there was a problem. So Nairobi and I had a problem between the 24th of October and the 6th of November. Now, said Mr. Lily, we come to November 13th. Were you due in court that day? Yes, answered Mr. Free, and what was the purpose of that asked Mr. Lily.

Well, said Mr. Free, there was a lot of motions that had been filed. You're talking about the pro se motions. Yes, answered Mr. Free that Nairobi Teasley filed on his own behalf. And they were scheduled to be heard on that day, is that correct?

Yes, said Mr. Free, I arrived at Judge Nail's courtroom around ten o'clock. I checked with the courtroom people, then I went upstairs because it was communicated to me by the deputies that Nairobi Teasley was **refusing** to come down to the courtroom.

All right, said Mr. Lily, on November 13 you have talked to Nairobi Teasley upstairs, and at some point during the course of that morning who was it who first spoke to you about these so-called threats? I believe in the Judge's office. When I say we, I'm talking now Judge Nail, myself, Mr. Tiger, I think, Mr. Wink was there as well, but I'm not sure about that. And Mr. How would have been there, also.

Was the judge through with his docket at the time you had the meeting, asked Mr. Lily?

I don't recall, said Mr. Free.

After you heard this threatening information Mr. Free, did you go up and talk to Nairobi Teasley? Sure, well, first we had to find him. He was. They bring prisoners over from the Justice Center by way of that overpass between the Justice Center and this building. He was refusing to answer to the role call when they called for him up there. That's what I discovered when I got up there. They finally had to take all the prisoners out of that part of the holding area up there and they eventually found him behind a bench or something, where he couldn't be seen. I didn't talk to him about the so-called threats. I talked to him about the wisdom of coming down so he could be there when his motions were heard, after all, they were his motions.

So Nairobi was not brought down at all that day, was he? asked Mr. Lily.

Mr. Free lied and said "and once we found him, at that point he was brought down." Nairobi was not in curt on November 13, 1997.

It seems to me that I probably could have done a better job had I not had to have the distraction, if you will, about having to worry about security issues, said Mr. Free. Would you say that the hindrance to your work was sufficient to have rendered your assistance ineffective asked Mr. Lily.

Mr. Free answered, what rendered my assistance less than totally effective. Mr. Mansfield, was Nairobi Teasley's unwillingness to work any counsel in his own behalf. That philosophy was conveyed to him by two people, Regenia Teasley and John Teasley.

His loyalty to his family was stronger than his loyalty, I think to get himself the best help he could. It's unfortunate, because he lost, in my opinion a **winnable case.**

2493.02 Arraignment

An accused person shall be arraigned by the Clerk of the Court of Common Pleas, or his deputy, reading the indictment or information to the accused, unless the accused or his attorney waives the reading thereof. He shall then be asked to plead thereto. Arraignment shall be made immediately after the disposition of exceptions to the indictment, if any are filed, or if no exceptions are filed after reasonable opportunity has been given the accused to file such exception.

2941.07 Bill of Particulars.

Upon written request of the defendant, made not later than five days prior to the date set for trial, or upon order of the court, the prosecuting attorney shall furnish a bill of particulars setting up specifically the nature of the offense charged and the conduct of the defendant which is alleged to constitute the offense.

2945.71 time within which hearing or trial must be held.

Within ninety days after his arrest or the service of summons, if the offense charged is a misdemeanor of the first or second degree, or other misdemeanor for which the maximum penalty is imprisonment for more than sixty day.

Trials for felony
Time limit generally equals 270 days
Time limit when accused confined in lieu of bail equals 90 days

2945.58 Alibi

Whenever a defendant in a criminal cause proposes to offer in his defense testimony to establish an alibi on his behalf, such defendant shall not less than three days before the trial of such cause file and serve upon the prosecuting attorney a notice in writing of his intention to claim such alibi. Notice shall include specific information as to the place at which the defendant claims to have been at the time of the alleged offense. If the defendant fails to file such written notice, the court may exclude evidence offered by the defendant for the purpose of proving such alibi.

2921.44 Dereliction of Duty

No law enforcement officer shall negligently do any of the following:

1. Fail to serve a lawful warrant without delay.

2921.45 Interfering with civil rights

A. No public servant, under color of his office, employment, or authority, shall knowingly deprive, or conspire or attempt to deprive any person of a constitutional or statutory right.

B. Whoever violates this section is guilty of interfering with civil rights, a misdemeanor of the first degree.

2941.45 Motion to quash

A motion to quash may be made when there is a defect apparent upon the face of the record, within the meaning of section 2941.02 to 2941.35 inclusive of the Revised Code, including defects in the form of indictment and in the manner in which an offense is charged.

2941.55 Pleas in abatement

Plea in abatement may be made when there is a defect in the record shown by facts extrinsic thereto.

2937.21 Continuance

<u>No</u> continuance at any stage of the proceeding, including that for determination of a motion, shall extend for more than 10 days unless **both** the state and the accused consent thereto. Any continuance or delay in ruling contrary to the provisions of this section shall, unless procured by defendant or his counsel, be grounds for discharge of the defendant forthwith.

THE DEFENSELESS, SENSELESS...DEFENSE

An appeal was filed in the Court of Appeals First Appellate District of Hamilton County, Ohio, by Mr. Lily. Mr. Lily was hired to file an appeal, but upon entering the contract we knew **not** of his illness.

Judgment from the court came back...Affirmed, Judgment, Entry, on appeal was April 30, 1999.

Nairobi nor his family knew of this decision.

And around the first week of June the family received a letter from Mr. Lily's law firm stating Mr. Lily was ill and his son would be handling his cases.

This was not true. So we had less than two weeks to find an attorney that would file Nairobi's appeal in the Supreme Court of Ohio.

I called around, no one wanted to help. Then I remembered Mr. Haa. I called, he said hold on, I have an attorney that will work with you. He put me on hold. While I was holding on Whitney was singing.

Mr. Gall, came to the phone. He made an appointment. He quoted his fee, and he quickly filed the papers needed to keep the defenseless lamb going. He as well as Nairobi's family knew nothing would be done. But we must keep trying. The Supreme Court refused to hear this case. Mr. Gall filed a post conviction for Nairobi. He knew that it was untimely, but Mr. Lily was in Utah, because of his cancer.

This also was refused, but it was refused by Judge Nail.   Mr. Gall filed an appeal on the decision made by Judge Nail.

This appeal came upon the calendar on August 9, 2000. This decision we are waiting for.

Regenia McQueen-Teasley

ABOUT THE AUTHOR

In my book *Nairobi Teasley, One Hour 30 Minutes Defenseless...Lamb*, I was motivated to write this book about the unfair treatment given Nairobi, my youngest son, as well as Nairobi's brother John Jr, and myself.

These are things that happened to John Jr. and myself for trying to support Nairobi and his defense.

I was born in Summerville, South Carolina. My husband John Sr. and I have five children: John Jr., Tonya, Ieichia, Nairobi and Rhodesia. I am the proud grandmother of twelve grandchildren. Raphael, Jamila, William, Nairobi Jr., Randi, De Jong, Donnish, Nairobi McQueen, Nyasij McQueen, Indonesia McQueen, Khydesia McQueen. In addition to being a homemaker, I am an author and have held various office positions.